THE
FUNDAMENTALS
OF ANIMATION

Fairchild Books
An imprint of Bloomsbury Publishing Plc

Imprint previously known as AVA Publishing

50 Bedford Square	1385 Broadway
London	New York
WC1B 3DP	NY 10018
UK	USA

www.bloomsbury.com

**FAIRCHILD BOOKS, BLOOMSBURY and the Diana logo
are trademarks of Bloomsbury Publishing Plc**

First published by AVA Publishing SA, 2005
This 2nd edition is published by Fairchild Books, an imprint of
Bloomsbury Publishing Plc
Copyright © Bloomsbury Publishing Plc, 2016

Paul Wells and Samantha Moore have asserted their right under the Copyright,
Designs and Patents Act, 1988, to be identified as Authors of this work.

British Library Cataloguing-in-Publication Data
A catalogue record for this book is available from the British Library.

ISBN: PB: 978-1-4725-7526-5
      ePDF: 978-1-4725-7527-2

Library of Congress Cataloging-in-Publication Data
Wells, Paul, 1961-
  The fundamentals of animation / Paul Wells and Samantha Moore.
     pages cm
  Includes bibliographical references and index.
  ISBN 978-1-4725-7526-5 (alk. paper) — ISBN 978-1-4725-7527-2 (alk. paper)
  1. Animated films. I. Moore, Samantha (Filmmaker) II. Title.
  NC1765.W43 2015
  791.43'34—dc23
                          2014047094
Series: Fundamentals

Cover design: Louise Dugdale
Cover image: Beryl and letters courtesy Joanna Quinn/BAF/
National Media Museum

Designed and Typeset by Saxon Graphics Ltd, Derby
Printed and bound in China

THE FUNDAMENTALS
OF ANIMATION

SECOND EDITION

Paul Wells and Samantha Moore

Fairchild Books
An imprint of Bloomsbury Publishing PLC

BLOOMSBURY
LONDON · OXFORD · NEW YORK · NEW DELHI · SYDNEY

Contents

Contexts   **198**

Introduction

'The art challenges the technology and the technology inspires the art. Technical artists are coming from computer graphic schools, and learning sculpture, drawing and painting, and traditional artists are learning more about technology. The more we get their cross-pollination the more we will stretch the boundaries of this medium.'

John Lasseter[1]

Animation and Popular culture

—

Animation is one of the most prominent aspects of popular culture worldwide. It informs every aspect of the visual terrain that surrounds us every day. It is present in its traditional form in the films produced by Disney, PIXAR, Dreamworks and Ghibli, and in television sit-coms like *The Simpsons* and *South Park*. Equally, it exhibits its versatility in every ad break, as anything from washing machines to cereal packets take on the characteristics of human beings and persuade us to buy them. Computer-generated (CG) animation finds close affiliation with the computer games industry. Most websites have some form of animated figure or banner, as well as housing new forms of cartoon; and on mobile devices, too, animated characters and games proliferate. As well as all this, independent animated film survives in the face of economic adversity, providing festivals with inventive and affecting shorts, while the 'invisible art' of animation within the special effects tradition carries on transforming, and in some aspects eradicating, 'live action' in blockbuster features. Animation also continues to embrace new applications in science, architecture, healthcare and broadcast journalism, to name but a few. Animation is simply everywhere.

This is no surprise. Animation is the most dynamic form of expression available to creative people. Animation is a cross-disciplinary and interdisciplinary art and craft, embracing drawing, sculpture, model-making, performance, dance, computer science, social science and much more. It has a distinctive language that enables it to create the art of the impossible. Whatever can be imagined can be achieved. This unique vocabulary can be used in a variety of different ways – for example, traditional drawn or cel, CG, or stop-motion animation – but crucially, whatever technique is used (and there are many more) it can service works from the most outlandish of cartoons to the most abstract of avant-garde films, and all else in between. This is why animation has remained the most consistently experimental art form even as it has entered the mass popularity of mainstream visual culture.

Animation continually offers new possibilities narratively, aesthetically and technically, encouraging new animators, artists and practitioners to explore new kinds of storytelling, to create new graphic and illustrative styles, and to use both traditional and new tools in the execution of their work. This book will address all of these aspects, seeking to be a useful primer in the 'how to' of animation across a number of disciplines, but also considering a range of critical ideas and historical perspectives that are pertinent to creative work of this kind.

Liz Faber and Helen Walters suggest that animation may be found 'occupying a space between film-making, art and graphic design',[2] while veteran animator Gene Dietch offers a more technically determined view, suggesting that frame-by-frame cinematic animation is 'the recording of individually created phases of imagined action in such a way as to achieve the illusion of motion when shown at a constant, predetermined rate, exceeding that of human persistence of vision'.[3] Much of the 'particularity' of animation, though, is in all the work that must be done before it becomes a film or digital presentation. Animated 'movement' is artificially created and not recorded from the real world. Consequently, animation almost intrinsically hides its process, and the 'art' that characterises that process. Only the outcome is important in the public imagination; however, for the prospective animator the core work is in the process, and it is that which is reflected throughout the rest of this book.

In many ways, when animation is made in the traditional frame-by-frame form it is comparatively easy to define, but this is significantly problematised in the digital era. Comics artist and theorist Scott McCloud has suggested that 'as the technological distinctions between media fall away, their conceptual distinctions will become more important than ever'.[4] This book, then, seeks to combine the traditional and orthodox ideas at the heart of animation with the 'bright new dawn' of the impact of the digital era, offering case studies and advice from artists, scholars and practitioners. In this book there is no difference between theory and practice – they are one and the same, as actually, they always have been. You cannot be a good animator, or indeed, an artist of any sort, without embracing historical perspectives and critical insight, all of which are embedded in any forward-thinking and original practical work.

It is likely that the 21st-century animation practitioner – you – is interested in and engaged with the visual dynamics of popular culture: comics; graphic novels; animé; pop promos; advertising; websites dedicated to left-field interests; cult TV and movies; fan cultures; contemporary modern art; and any aspect of visual culture that has entered into the mainstream of the popular imagination by the time this book has been published. For the most part, all creative people start off as 'fans' of something and want to make something like the art they admire. These are the catalysts for animators wanting to emulate a particular style or approach, while at the same time trying to find an individual 'voice'.

It is likely, too, that many contemporary animators have found access to the medium through increasingly affordable software packages, and the trial and error of making animation in back-bedroom 'studios'. Animators with no formal training have been able to use inexpensive computer programs to create quality work without a colossal budget or using the extensive film crews present in the credits of major movies. Further, college and university courses have proliferated to accommodate the increasing interest in animation, and there is training available in traditional and CG animation.

Inevitably, in a global culture so aware of the works of the PIXAR and Dreamworks studios, and so invested in computer games, there is high creative aspiration among fledgling practitioners, but a note of caution also needs to be added. As Bill Fleming has noted, 'The problem with technology is it can greatly simplify some tasks while greatly complicating others … In 2D, the animator simply draws the body perfectly and doesn't have to worry about the technology getting in the way or falling short. Being a digital animator means also being a technical engineer and in many cases a programmer.'[5] So, making choices is crucial – what is the best approach for you, your ideas, your abilities and your ambitions? This book will try and help you make those choices.

Animation offers extraordinary versatility and range in its style and techniques, but there are some fundamental principles at its heart that distinguish it as an art form, a practical craft, and a distinctive means of expression. It is hoped that the following discussion will highlight those principles by engaging with the process in developing an animated film; defining the multiple roles and perspectives in thinking about the use and execution of animation; and through the advice and support offered by a range of case studies in which students and professionals making animated films in a variety of contexts speak critically about their projects, and share 'best practice'. At a time when there is an increasing number of books about animation – and any number of 'making of' documentaries available, concerned with technical considerations, historical perspective, creative outcomes and critical analysis – it is crucial that these aspects are not seen as separate, but part of the same approach. The whole point of this discussion, therefore, is to keep these perspectives working together in a book that we hope will be thought provoking and practical, and, ultimately, fundamentally useful to the critically engaged, creative practitioner.

Why Animation?

—

Why choose animation instead of live action? There are many possible answers to this question, but the following points may serve to summarise some of the key perspectives:

- Animation offers a different vocabulary of expression to live action and enables greater creative freedoms.

- Animation gives a greater degree of control over the construction and outcome of the work.

- Animation may be usefully related to and operate within the physical and material world of live action.

- Animation can offer a different representation of 'reality' or create worlds governed by their own codes and conventions that radically differ from the 'real world'.

- Animation can achieve anything that can be imagined and create an 'art of the impossible'.

All these perspectives acknowledge distinctiveness in the form, which may be recognised in all its approaches and disciplines. The process by which an animated film might be made, though, is variable. It has some generic consistencies, but often varies with the technique employed, the purpose of the project and its outcome and, crucially, as a result of the working methods employed by an individual or a collaborative team. The 'process' guide shown here, therefore, is only one model of an approach to practice, but it encompasses many of the core aspects required.

The Animation Process

Concept: the inciting idea
Independent project/Studio project/Commercial commission
Creating schedule of work
Budget/Planning/Timeframe
Reviewing resources
Technique/Technical needs/Team involved
Research
Facilitating the idea
Story
Narrative/Dramatic scenarios/Comic events
Preparatory visualisation
Sketches/Models
Formal design
Characters/Costume/Contexts/Conditions
Storyboard
Thumbnail version/Reference version/
Fixed version
Script
Descriptions/Dialogue
Vocal performance/Initial soundtrack
Animatic

Shooting script
Animation analysis
Executing action/Performance/Effects
Aesthetic analysis
Colour/Style/Materials
Layout
Cinematic considerations
Dope sheet
Construction and execution
Development soundtrack
Backgrounds/Sets/Virtual contexts
Animation sequences
Movement tests/Blocking decisions
Creating sequences
Using film language
Construction
Combining elements
Post-production analysis
Final mix/Edit
Output to chosen format
Exhibition

It's important to recognise that this is not a strict linear process. Many aspects of the production process overlap and become subject to the ups and downs of creative practice. Things do go wrong and need to be recovered; aspects of any production are constantly reviewed and revised as they go along; and things that seem hard and fast can quickly be jettisoned in preference to another idea or in response to a pragmatic concern. One key point remains though, and that is the importance of pre-production, as we'll see in Chapter 1.

NOTES

1. J. Lasseter, quoted in the PIXAR Animation Masterclass, London Film Festival, National Film Theatre, November 2001.
2. L. Faber and H. Walters, *Animation Unlimited: Innovative Short Films Since 1940* (London: Laurence King Publishing, 2004), p. 6.
3. Cited in S. Withrow, *Toon Art: The Graphic Art of Digital Cartooning* (Lewes: Ilex, 2003), p. 11.
4. S. McCloud, *Reinventing Comics* (New York: Paradox Books, 2000), p. 205.
5. Quoted in Withrow, *Toon Art*, p. 54.

PART

Principles
and Processes

Being pragmatic and practical at the pre-production stage will enable the project to succeed because there is the opportunity to prepare for its demands. While it is vital that the animator is imaginative, it is equally vital to know how that which is imagined can be realised.

Pre-production – the preparation of the essential resources and materials to make and complete a project – is an often undervalued part of making animated films. Pre-production begins right from the initial idea and must always be informed by a clear understanding of where the budget will come from; how much time there is; how the work will be conducted; and how the idea itself will translate into a high-quality animation, with, hopefully, some originality.

In every pre-production process there is challenge and difficulty, but if mistakes are to be made and learned from, it is best that they take place during this period of preparation. Refining the idea through the initial script development and visualisation process is crucial, as is getting a real sense of how the story will be actually executed in relation to its technique.

Ideas Generation

Often one of the most difficult aspects of doing any piece of creative work is finding an idea that has genuine potential for an original film, and the worst thing that anyone can do is place a piece of blank paper in front of someone and say 'write' or 'draw'.

Paul Driessen is one of the acknowledged masters of animation and one of the most distinctive film-makers in the field. Aside from his signature visual style, the key strength of Driessen's films is their conceptual focus – the inciting idea that informs the making of the film.

What follows, then, is a range of starting points for ideas, supported by some individual examples and comments by Driessen himself. While clearly geared to a personal film-making agenda, these approaches are also suitable for responding to a commercial brief, or as a story development process within the body of a bigger narrative process.]

Methods of Recording

—

The context in which an animator may try to generate ideas may be important, and the method by which these initial musings are stirred and recorded is crucial at the beginning of the process. Some artists prefer to write stories in prose; others to generate any number of stimulus sketches; some work from bullet-pointed conceptual thoughts or odd notes made over a period of time. The 'starting place' is rarely a mystical moment of the muse descending; it tends to be an accumulation of developing thought and trial and error until an inciting idea – which must also be 'an exciting idea' – emerges, which has sufficient substance to be pursued further.

Driessen: 'I do not draw my stories at this stage, but I write them down. I can vaguely picture in my head what it will look like, but there is no definite image yet. Writing is abstract. I'm not hampered by design. Writing also goes much faster than drawing and one can insert afterthoughts and correct flaws, without spending time on draughtsmanship, however sketchy. But it does depend on how your mind works, the kind of stories you write, your style and experience within that approach. Some people need doodling, need to see images to find clues and directions. Eventually, I do make a storyboard. It suggests the look of the film and defines, more or less, the various shots, the progress and order of the action.'

Using personal backgrounds

—

Our biggest resource in the first instance is ourselves, and thinking about our backgrounds and the characters and possible narratives that inform them is a ready place to generate possible material. Many creative works have a strong autobiographical tendency because the artist has such in-depth knowledge on the subject and can transform it into a set of aesthetic and social, as well as personal, outcomes.

Using personal experiences and memory

—

Using personal experience and memory is, of course, intrinsically related to drawing upon background, but it needs to be subjected to a rigorous process of interrogation. It is important to observe more objectively; analyse incident and experience structurally; and treat the things that happen as possibilities for narrative and other forms of expression.

Sense memories

—

Everyone has an 'emotional' memory that is built on our five senses – seeing, hearing, smelling, touching and tasting. Recalling when we saw something beautiful or tragic, heard a particular piece of music, smelt a potent odour or fragrance, touched something or someone, or tasted something delicious may be the key catalyst to a prospective story idea. Using the senses is fundamental to the animator's craft, as these have to be projected through the medium in highly specific and connective ways.

The formative years

—

Many artists of all kinds are influenced by the creative work of their youth. Long-term personal likes and dislikes are often the first things that are emulated or aspired to in creative work before a clear and original 'voice' develops. These influences can be conscious or unconscious.

Using iconic images

—

Contemporary culture is a visual one. We are surrounded by visual stimulus in images, signs and pictorial information, as well as the physical environment itself. Sometimes particular images and signs take on an 'iconic' value and pass into popular culture as situations and scenarios that are known to a mass population, and these can be used as the foundation of further interpretation or development.

Driessen: 'Just imagine a cabin sitting on a railway track in the middle of nowhere. Then make a list of everything that has to do with the railways, the era of locomotives, whatever comes to mind, and stories and gags start to emerge from that imagery.'

Fantasy versus reality: observation and imagination

—

Everyone is blessed with the ability to fantasise – to reimagine the world on our own terms and conditions, fulfilling our innermost passions and desires. Most people realise that their fantasies are often in stark contrast to the real world in which they live. This juxtaposition can be very fruitful for the artist, as acute observation of the patterns of the real world, set against a free imagination unfettered by rules, regulation and convention, can produce interesting points of comparison. This can set off potent ideas for personal expression.

Using oppositions and comparisons

—

Similar to the tensions between reality and fantasy, the self-evident points of comparison and opposition between people, other creatures, the environment etc., can enable a 'dramatic conflict' that can generate ideas. Creating a particular tension or problem that must be resolved is a fundamental aspect of many narratives and often emerges from the dramatic conflict of opposition or difference.

Driessen: '[For *On Land, At Sea and in the Air*] I had made a lot of notes about comparable situations. Like hills and valleys, fire, water and soil; aggression versus peace; complementary colours etc. The moment I had established the land, sea and air environments, I added the themes influencing each segment, like rain, hunger, love, up and down, and the stories almost evolved from there by themselves. I learned that whenever I hit upon a good premise for a film, the stories would follow without much effort.'

Using and revising traditional story premises

—

Most people are brought up hearing stories, reading stories and creating stories about their own lives and experiences. People are highly attuned to the capacity for narrative, and every day they express their inner life, the things that happen to them and to others as 'stories', built on an instinctive structure of a beginning, a middle and an end. There are some key story ideas and structures that we retain from popular narratives – these can work as very effective stimuli for developing the stories further.

Driessen: 'Another film I tried out on my students was a story exercise (after I'd done it myself) – *Oh, What a Knight*. It has a typical cartoon premise. As a start I used a traditional tale – the knight rescuing a damsel in distress. We all know the outcome, the knight will overcome all obstacles and eventually free her. But then what? What will make the end funny? Using the same structure, I gave the students exercises with traditional story ideas like "a woman being tied to the railway track and a cowboy coming to the rescue", "someone falling off the roof and her neighbour trying to catch her in time", "Snow White threatened by her stepmother and the dwarves coming to the rescue".'

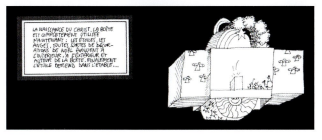

1.1

Storyboard for *The Old Box* – Paul Driessen

Driessen drew from personal memories to find a narrative that would also be suitable to try out new aspects of working in the animated form.

1.2

**Still and a storyboard from *The Boy Who Saw the Iceberg* —
Paul Driessen**

In choosing the split screen device for *The Boy Who Stole the Iceberg*, Driessen wanted to show two parallel realities: 'In this case, the little boy's fantasies, his means to indulge in wild adventures, next to his real, boring life.' This set the pattern for the story, creating drama from the comparison of the unfolding narratives.

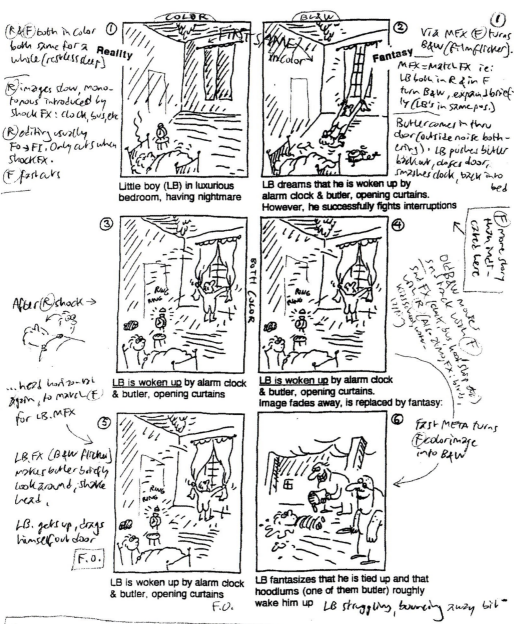

(R&F) both in color ①
both same for a
while (restless sleep) **Reality**

(R) images slow, mono-
tonous introduced by
shock FX: clock, bus, etc

(R) editing usually
FO → FI. Only cuts when
shock FX.

(F) fast cuts

COLOR

E FIRST SAME

Little boy (LB) in luxurious
bedroom, having nightmare

② Via MFX (F) turns
B&W (Film flicker).

MFX = Match FX ie:
LB both in R & in F
turn B&W, expand brief-
ly (LB's in same pos.)

Butler comes in thru
door (outside noise both-
ering). LB pushes butler
back out, closes door,
smashes clock, back into
bed

BLW

in Color **Fantasy**

LB dreams that he is woken up by
alarm clock & butler, opening curtains.
However, he successfully fights interruptions

③

After (R) shock →

... head horizontal
again, to match (F)
for LB. MFX

RING
RING

BOTH COLOR

LB is woken up by alarm clock
& butler, opening curtains

④

(F) more story
than met-
cards here

die B&W moves (F)
shock will
sm. FX (carts bus, last close &c)
and FR. (alu-ching FX, birds)
small R. ...
noises, when
bird ...

LB is woken up by alarm clock
& butler, opening curtains.
Image fades away, is replaced by fantasy:

⑤

LB.FX (B&W flicker)
makes butler barely
look around, shake
head.

LB. gets up, drags
himself out door

F.O.

RING
RING

LB is woken up by alarm clock
& butler, opening curtains
F.O.

⑥ Fast META turns
(F) color image
into B&W

LB fantasizes that he is tied up and that
hoodlums (one of them butler) roughly
wake him up   LB struggling, bouncing away bit

NOTE: After (R) shock brings LB back to reality,
reality images in color usually continue for
a while on both sides / Till F. sets in again.

17

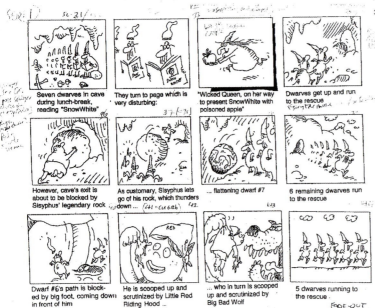

Seven dwarves in cave during lunch-break, reading "SnowWhite"

They turn to page which is very disturbing:

"Wicked Queen, on her way to present SnowWhite with poisoned apple"

Dwarves get up and run to the rescue

However, cave's exit is about to be blocked by Sisyphus' legendary rock

As customary, Sisyphus lets go of his rock, which thunders down ...

... flattening dwarf #7

6 remaining dwarves run to the rescue

Dwarf #6's path is blocked by big foot, coming down in front of him

He is scooped up and scrutinized by Little Red Riding Hood ...

... who in turn is scooped up and scrutinized by Big Bad Wolf

5 dwarves running to the rescue

FADE-OUT

1.3

Sketch and storyboards from *Three Misses* — Paul Driessen

Much later in his career, looking for a fun cartoon idea for a new film, Driessen used the very story exercises he had undertaken with his students to combine three popular narratives: 'I designed the film as a series of cliff-hangers; at the moment of tension I would cut to the next story and so on. I also inserted some reminders of previous action into the subsequent stories: the apartment man closes a door behind which Little Red Riding Hood, the wolf and the unfortunate dwarf are seen; and the falling-off-the-roof lady is passed by the cowboy jumping off the cliff.'

Research and the Pre-production Process

Research is an important yet undervalued component of animation. It may require visits to the library, real locations and places of visual stimulus; you might need time online, primary material, people to interview or access to documents or images not in the public domain. Research is the next step in developing the initial concept.

Pre-production research must also include technical planning: Can the software used facilitate what is required? Is the resource available appropriate, useful and able to achieve the outcomes imagined? Research is necessary in any number of ways, because it properly informs the project in relation to both form and content.

Research and Development: *Jurassic Park*

—

Here Ellen Poon, one of the senior animators at Industrial Light and Magic (ILM) talks about the detailed research process in the development of Steven Spielberg's blockbuster *Jurassic Park* (Universal Studios, 1993).

Poon: I do not think that there is a limit to what our imagination can create, and the classic cartoons proved that. What we are trying to do at ILM is to push the boundaries and create something that we have not seen before. With *Jurassic Park* we tried to use models to do the animation at the start, but the movement turned out to be insufficiently fluid to be persuasive, so we did a test and built some dinosaurs that we could scan into the computer.

'We did some animation of *T. rex*, and there was a strong sense that these were real animals moving around. You can combine these computer-generated elements with live action in the computer environment so they seem wholly realistic and indistinguishable. First, we had to consider the movement of the creature; second, we had to consider the look and texture of those creatures because they have to look and act like animals – they have to breathe and sweat like real animals; and third, they must be as persuasive as the live-action environment.

'The animators studied a lot of live-action footage of animals running around – maybe feeding or hunting – just studying the movement to get some idea of the spirit and character of the animal. Also, they did some mime classes when they actually had to become a dinosaur and actually establish a character. By trying to understand the spirit of the creature they can try and put that into the animation.

'Like the character development in any movie, you can see the progression from when the creature is introduced, to how it interacts with the live-action actors and actresses, and how it behaves. This helps with making sure that the animation of the creature matches the stage of development they should be at, at the particular moment within the story. This has to work alongside the technical issues like lighting, or creating skin tone, or authenticating the texture of the creature.

'We did a lot of research on skin movement in animals. We shot a lot of the live-action scenes with objects moving around in the environment, so we could create lighting diagrams, which helped us to make sure that everything looked right when the dinosaurs moved in and out of shade; basically that they were never anything but part of the environment.'

Preparation

—

The visualisation of an animated film is the key component in thinking about how a story might be told, how a visual 'gag' might be constructed, how a technique might be applied, and how the animation will work as a piece of film. Drawing underpins this process of visualisation.

Drawing, however primitive or sophisticated, and for whatever technique, is a necessary process. Drawing can work in a number of ways and is an intrinsic skill everyone possesses. All children draw and are totally unselfconscious about it. As the years pass, though, the belief that we all can draw is somehow socialised out of us and is merely understood as an 'artistic' skill.

Simply, any act of sketching offers up a perception of the world, and a model by which to communicate thoughts and feelings and a range of sensory experience. It can enable the invention of a world by asking questions of the one we all live in. Primarily, though, drawing records the act of observation – a key skill in the animator's armoury – and sometimes it is an act of memory, in the recollection of times and places of significance.

All drawing affords the possibility, though, of experimentation and interpretation, and works as core research in developing a vocabulary of human movements and gestures; an understanding of environments; the invention of fantastical figures and places; or simply, the expression of line, form, shape and colour, for its own sake.

Life drawing

—

Master animator Joanna Quinn, creator of *Girls Night Out* and *Body Beautiful*, discusses how she works as an example of good practice.

Quinn: 'Life drawing and drawing from life is an essential part of my animation. Even though people say I'm a good "drawer" and have a good understanding of three-dimensional movement, I still need to draw from life. If I don't, my drawings become flat and timid. When I'm doing a lot of observational drawing outside of my animation, my line becomes a lot more confident and I think three-dimensionally.

'I carry a sketchbook around with me and draw at every opportunity. I use my sketchbook as a visual notebook and the drawings are interpretations of what I'm looking at.

'Yesterday I sketched a man reading his newspaper in the doctor's surgery. The pose looked a familiar one, i.e., slumped over, leaning forward with the paper, arms resting on legs. When I looked closer, I couldn't believe how hunched over he was and his head hung so low his torso was almost doubled up. His feet were interesting too, one foot forward and the other pulled back under his chair. If I'd drawn this pose from my imagination I would never have exaggerated it as much, which is exactly why it is so important to draw from life. We may think our imaginations are far more adventurous than real life, but for me truth is always stranger than fiction.'

2.1

Jurassic Park – Steven Spielberg

Jurassic Park was successful in creating authentic creatures both in relation to the computer animation used, and the research that underpinned the plausible movement and behaviour of the dinosaurs. Audiences needed to relate to recognisable 'animals' even though they would have never encountered such beasts.

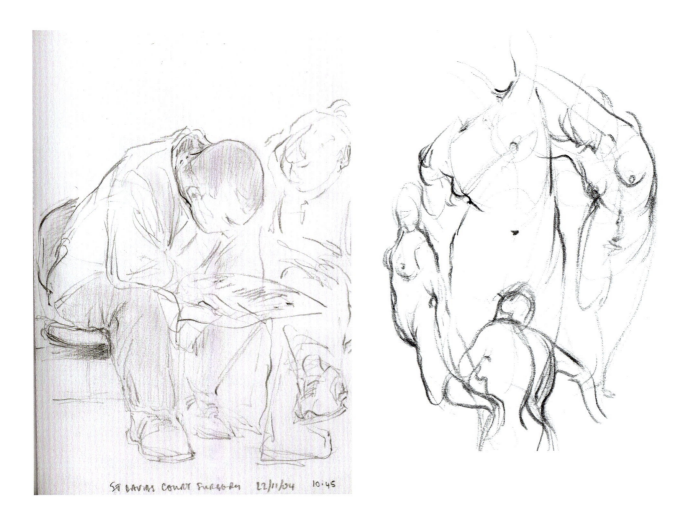

St Davins Court Surgery   22/11/04   10.45

2.2

The importance of sketching – Joanna Quinn

Drawing from life often discovers more
exaggerations in postures than those imagined,
as this hunched man seen in a doctor's surgery
shows. Quinn makes an important distinction
when she suggests 'my drawings are purely
interpretations of what I am looking at, rather
than being aesthetically good drawings'.
Inexperienced artists can often be inhibited in
their expression and vision by thinking that their
drawings are insufficiently 'artistic' or falling
short of a certain standard.

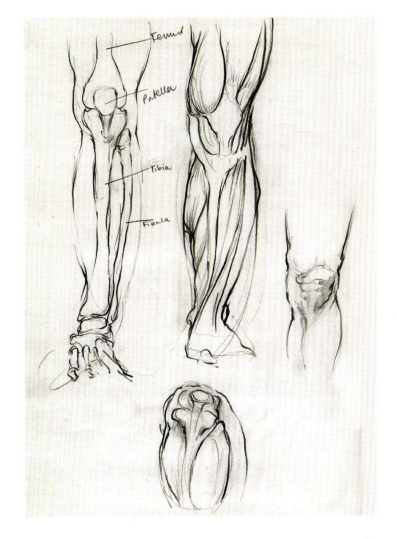

Inspiration and Visualisation

—

The Tannery is a 2D short animated film made in 2010, directed by Iain Gardner and produced by Axis Animation and Digicult. It has won prizes internationally and was long-listed for the 'Best Animated Short Film' Academy Award in 2011.

Using drawing (sketching, painting, collage) to create the tone and feel of the film, as well as the narrative thread, is key. Drawing develops from being a record of an event or thought into a way of communicating complex ideas to an audience. Gardner says, 'I come up with ideas conceptually and then guide them through images. If there's no concept behind a drawing then it doesn't expand any further; it just becomes a nice study.'

While developing the initial images for *The Tannery* Gardner drew on different influences for visual inspiration. He had always loved the illustration work of Czech animator Jiří Trnka and was inspired by the fairy-tale quality of Trnka's work, as well as the winter scenes from the film *Bambi* (Disney, 1942).

Ideas for animated shorts are often a blend of a conceptual idea with a strong visual image. Gardner said that the idea for *The Tannery* was inspired by an anecdote he heard from a friend about their granny's fur stole, which had apparently spontaneously combusted. Iain said, 'I just got this image in my head that the ghost of the animal whose skin it was had been responsible for that, that it wanted its property back.' He scribbled the idea down on a scrap of paper – 'I remember thinking; I must log this, and it was just a little note, stuffed in my pocket' – and the seed of the idea was planted.

The idea gestated for a couple of years, and eventually surfaced as a film script for a funding bid, which was significantly edited through various incarnations to the version that was finally made. The central concept always stayed true to that original idea, though, and drawing thumbnails, storyboarding sequences and colour treatments were vital in the process. The colour palette and style of the film were established early on: 'There was a story in my head and there were sequences I could imagine that excited me and drove the project forward,' Gardner said.

He played with the designs of the animals in sketches and watercolour paint. It was important to delineate between the 'real' animals and their spirit versions. For the design of the animal spirits he started thinking about negative images of the living characters: 'The ghost characters were basically inversions of the warm colours of the live animals.'

Gardner plans his films physically on paper first. He finds working straight onto a digital tablet restrictive, as some of his layouts for *The Tannery* were very large. He likes to use physical materials to make images, and for the animal characters he wanted to capture the hand-drawn line before it was scanned digitally and treated. For the opening chase sequence he worked with Axis Animation, who animated the forest landscape in 3D wireframe. Iain then printed out the frames to animate the hand-drawn characters over the top, ensuring that the film retained his hand-drawn style.

The film uses no dialogue; as Gardner explains, 'My affinity is for music and dance. I think visually and sometimes find the construct of a script limiting … if words on a page can convey the effect I'm trying to get across in a movement then why animate it? … It's the emotion you're trying to get across to an audience.'

2.3

Capturing and developing an idea – *The Tannery*, Iain Gardner

The initial sketch of a fox, which inspired the film, and the preparatory sketchbook work that followed.

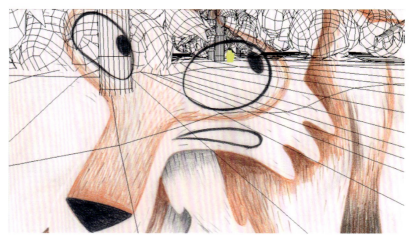

2.4

Planning and preparation – *The Tannery*, Iain Gardner

The preparatory movement study, character design work and print outs of the wireframe chase sequence with character drawings on top.

Concept Art and Design

—

Concept art as part of the pre-production process is a way of defining the overall look of the film and can be a crucial element of communicating the idea to a client or commissioner. It conveys the idea of the film through the medium used, colour palette chosen and mood evoked.

Richard Phelan graduated with an MA in animation direction from the National Film & Television School in 2011. During his time at the NFTS Richard directed his graduation film *Damned*, which won several awards, including a Royal Television Society Award. He worked as a storyboard artist at London studios Nexus and Framestore before moving to Aardman in Bristol to work on the children's television series *Shaun the Sheep*. Since then he has worked on commercials, television series and also written several episodes of *Shaun the Sheep*. Richard currently works as a features story artist and writer at Aardman Animations. His most recent project is the *Shaun the Sheep* movie (2015).

Phelan stresses how important it is to get your ideas clear before you start visualizing the project. He says, 'if it doesn't work, it doesn't work. It doesn't matter how beautiful it looks, if it doesn't work that just magnifies the problem.'

Phelan says that the important thing about concept art is the communication of your vision, especially to others. 'When I pitched *Damned* [his NFTS graduation film] ten different people had ten different ideas about how it was going to look. But when I showed them the concept art they were like "Ooooh! It's going to look like *that*!"… Concept art allows you to make concrete how it's going to look.'

It also helps to sell a tricky idea; if you are making a film with a very original look, or unusual technique, then it 'is your friend, because you're able to convey "proof of concept" as they call it in advertising'.

He describes it as a 'statement of intent' for your project, as the film-making process progresses: '[The idea] might change due to unforeseen circumstances, and it starts to muddy what you originally intended. [The concept art] tells you – don't forget this is what you were trying to do – because otherwise you can lose your way. Remind yourself what you were trying to do at the start.'

It can be a crucial part of pitching for a project: 'Concept art allows you to very cheaply and quickly see what the film will look like and see if it has legs … you can say, "Here's my cheap drawings, now give me some money to make the real thing!"'

Phelan also describes how using key images from the storyboard, worked up to concept art standard, can help to pinpoint issues in the flow of the film. '[At Aardman] there's a process that we use with very few images, called beat boards, outlining the high spots of the main character's journey. You're seeing if the story flows correctly and where the weak points are. And you're never reworking the weak point; you're changing something earlier on where something hasn't happened that needs to in order to make the story work further down the line.'

You can see more about beat boards in the section Storyboards and Narrative on page 36. Colour scripting, although it often comes later in the pre-production process, is another useful tool at the concept art stage. For example, a scene happening at night, in streetlight, will have a totally different feel to the same scene enacted in mid-afternoon. As Richard says: 'Colour scripting is a very quick way to give an emotional sense of the film, to give an idea of the journey taken over the duration of the film.'

He always envisaged his one-minute boxing film *Grit* in black and white: 'I like creative limitations … if money and time are no object then it becomes

bloated and self-indulgent.' Phelan based the look of the film on classic *Time Life* photos, with high contrast and dynamic movement. 'I just started playing with charcoal, adding pencil and paint', to replicate that graphic, stylized look of classic black and white photography.'

Working up the concept art in his sketchbook, Phelan says the one that really stuck out for him was the image of the boxer silhouetted against the light, bisected by

the boxing ring ropes. 'That image was the one that told me it was going to work. The others, some are working and some are not, but this one summed up my ideas about the concept driven by the sound – the world outside the ring and the world inside.'

2.5

Pre-production work from the short film *Grit*, directed by Richard Phelan

The images used here are concept art images from a project Richard did in the first year at the NFTS, where the students were given a one-minute piece of sound, without any context or consultation, and given the task of making animation to go with it. 'Students in the sound department each make one-minute tracks and we [animation direction students] pull them out at random … mine immediately sounded to me like boxing, it sounded like the inside of someone's head.'

2.6

'I like images which ask questions, like "Who's he?" Or "Why are we there?" When you really want to know, "What's he looking at?", then you can start to pull out your story'.

2.7

Phelan advocates getting opinions of people you trust to look at your work in progress at the pre-production stage – someone who can 'stop you going down a rabbit hole, say to you that you're getting too caught up in that aspect of the film'.

'The final image was built up of multiple layers, built up in After Effects, being much more experimental in approach and developing it on from the pencil line in the original sketches.'

Story and Design

—

Barry Purves is a master stop-motion animator with over 50 international awards for his films, which include *Screenplay*, *Rigoletto* and *Gilbert and Sullivan: The Very Models*. Here are some points from Purves to consider when designing animation:

■ Animators should try and engage with other art forms, particularly those that privilege movement, for example, dance; and those that tell stories by other means, for example, opera, through music.

■ Animation is basically an art of 'metaphor' and is perfect for all kinds of role-play to show different perspectives and ideas about the culture we live in.

■ 'Acting' is at the core of affecting animation, and it is particularly important to concentrate on body language and physical gesture as the tools of expression.

■ Make sure that your 'acting' through the figure is simple and clear – one simple gesture is better than five noisy ones.

■ Try not to move everything in every frame – pauses are beneficial and silences can be dramatically effective.

■ Not all animation should aspire to be 'realistic', but it should be credible. Establish the 'illogical logic' of the world you create and give it credibility.

■ Try to make sure that all the elements of your animated world are used to tell your story – for example, colour, design, lighting etc. – and that these elements are integrated in a coherent way.

■ Animation is a form of choreography, so don't just concentrate on the face and don't be afraid of showing your whole figure in the frame. Hold poses, stretch movement and change the rhythm – 25 frames do not have to be divided equally. Animation is not mathematics and there are no set laws.

■ Try to capture the 'essence' of your character's figure in the design, and build a specific vocabulary of movement for it, so that the 'meaning' in the acting will be clear and distinctive.

■ Embrace the artifice and illusionism of animation, so that you are able to create 'plays within plays' or 'films within films' to condense your plot, but, more importantly, to 'illuminate' a supposedly known or taken-for-granted world from a different perspective.

Design as Concept

—

Director, designer and co-producer (with Jim Turner) of the Pilsner Urquell commercial, Chris Randall from Second Home Studios, talked to us about making this ambitious production, which won a British Animation Award.

The agency allowed Second Home some flexibility visually. The design was partially based on medieval wood cuts, and the original Czech written proclamation was used in the droplets appearing and disappearing across the town. 'That was the biggest effects challenge, because we didn't exactly know how that was going to be done. That's when we came up with the idea of using these little templates, to create the tracking information for the ink spots to let the text fade in and out.'

2.8

Pilsner Urquell commercial – Chris Randall and Jim Turner
The brief for the stop-motion advert was 'Legends', celebrating the legacy and provenance of Pilsner Urquell and the craft of making it.

2.9

Green screen templates were used to give the effect of ink blots made from text.

'All in all we had about 16 motion control passes … we used about 3 or 4 beauty states, and different lighting states – each one with a different matte pass, all with different information to overlay. For the lightning we shot a whole pass flooded with light and then cut in those frames to allow us granular control over every aspect of the shoot.'

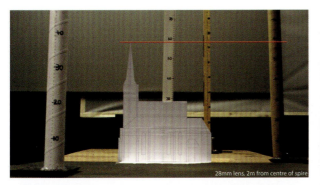

2.10
The whole camera move was governed by one key measurement – they used a cardboard mock-up of the cathedral to use for reference. 'We did a pre-visualisation of the camera move so that I knew that it worked and we knew the perimeters we were working within, and it gave everyone a point of reference.' The size of the cathedral also dictated the type of lens to use and then how big the green screen was.

The lead modeller, Sarra Hornby, did extensive research on all the different types of paper before she built the prototype barley stalk. They ended up making hundreds of barley stalks, 'covering all the shelves in the studio!' 'We opted for this Indian parchment paper called "khadi", which is hand pressed and really nice and thick … we had to do loads of R&D testing and ended up using lots of different types from heavy watercolour paper to thin translucent till roll paper.'

2.11
Around 25 people worked on the project for 13 weeks. The stalks alone took around two months to make by a team of modellers. They made the square first, then disassembled that and did the field scene.'

Chris says that it was the problem solving that was the most interesting for him while making this commercial. 'I'm most proud of the town square shot, because of the number of passes it took to complete it. I trained as a clapper loader on motion control shoots so I understood the principles, but I adapted what I already knew to make them work for this scenario.'

The scene where the plants are growing was all shot in reverse and composited together with the upward shot through the earth, which was shot forwards. 'Because it was all destructive you're timing it in your head backwards … you're conscious of how much you're cutting off each time and aware that you only have one go at it.'

Storyboards and Narrative

—

The key aspect of the visualisation process is storyboarding. Though this is intrinsically related to the script and soundtrack – considered later in this pre-production chapter – it is addressed here as a logical continuity of the drawing and design process. It is in the storyboard stage that visualisation is intrinsically linked to narrative – literally telling the story in pictures.

There can be three stages to the storyboarding process: a thumbnail version, created by one or more animators developing sequences; the reference version, which has a provisional, but agreed structure, with more detailed and larger drawings; and a fixed version, the final structured storyboard that is used in the 'animatic' or 'story reel', is correspondent to the provisional soundtrack and informs the finalisation of a shooting script. Depending upon the approach of individuals or studios this may vary, and – as it is important to continually stress – aspects of the process overlap and have different time frames.

PIXAR Animation Studios has a rigorous preparation process for its pictorial story development. Director Pete Docter and editor Lee Unkrich explain aspects of storyboarding.

Docter: 'We work off a "beat board". As we are developing the story, we pin a number of story "beats" – basic scene ideas, images, exchanges – on to a board and shuffle them around until we really get the essence of the story, what is the basic "plot". Sometimes we use blue cards to signal various character points – character attributes that we want to nail down. As we are doing this we are writing things down – developing a treatment, and beginning a script, just like you would in live action. This is just the starting point. But the key thing is fixing the storyboards, and then a story reel. Our Head of Story will "pitch" various sequences from this material to the staff, and if we think it is entertaining, we will film it on video, using the images, our own voices and special effects.'

EXPERT ADVICE

Chris Randall's tips for following a client brief:

- Try and stay flexible.
- Plan your project realistically, according to what's available to you.
- Give your client as many options as you can going in … but make sure they're as close to the brief as possible. Don't go too far off on a tangent unless you can justify it.
- Know when to say no and when to say yes – you can end up chasing your tail.
- If you're working alone you can get blinkered, so road test any ideas with another pair of fresh eyes before you go ahead.
- Clients may be doing a trawl to see what's out there – it's not an exam, there's no right answer.

Unkrich: 'We have a lot of fun getting a "pitch" like this to a live audience, but we are also deluding ourselves sometimes; some of the things we found funny were not so funny after a while, and maybe were not so funny in the story reel. A story reel is effectively a "rough draft" of the movie. We take all the storyboards and combine them with temporary dialogue that we record with employees at PIXAR, and we put in sound effects and music, and edit things together so that we create our "movie", and try and make it as watchable as the finished film that you go and see in the theatre. We spend a huge amount of time on this. A movie can take about five years to make, and only about a year and half of that is the actual animation. Our attitude is that if it is not working in the story reel then it is not suddenly going to magically get better because it has got pretty animation in it. If you get the story right, and the scenes are working well, then the animation will take it up to a whole other level.

'It is one of the real luxuries that we have over live action in that the story reel gives us the opportunity to see that "in-between state" between the script page and the finished film. Normally, you have your script – that's your bible; you go out and shoot it, and that's what you get. But we get to see if something is not working in advance.'[1]

Storyboards and Composition
—

Nelson Diplexcito is a film-maker and lecturer at Loughborough University, UK. He defines his film-making practice by its difference to traditional 'classical' narrative and also the expectations of 'abstraction' in avant-garde films. He insists that this is closely related to knowing the rules of composition and uses of space in the image frame, and breaking them for particular effects. Animators need to address this aspect of their work very consciously.

Diplexcito: 'Setting out to design pictures, animate images or direct movement will involve an understanding of compositional and spatial devices. The organisation of elements within the picture field, screen space or space within the frame is central in communicating the intention of the maker and the meaning of the work to the viewer.

'How do we begin to organise the space within the frame, and what is – and how do we achieve – effective composition? An effective composition is one that can be seen to communicate visual sense and directs the viewer's eye towards those aspects that the maker wants them to see. Visual sense is central in articulating the space within the frame and in communicating and directing the viewer to the meaning and reading of the work. I have outlined below considerations that may be helpful in attaining effective pictorial and visual sense in your storyboards. Some of these you will be familiar with, others will come to you intuitively and some you will begin to recognise through experimentation and visual practice.'

NOTE
1. Quoted in the PIXAR Animation Masterclass, London Film Festival, National Film Theatre, November 2001.

A concept and the appearance of reality
—

'The concept and the appearance of "reality" establish the framework for the compositional and spatial indicators within the picture field. The establishment of "the look" or the "texture of reality" can in turn communicate and underpin the concept. The concept and the appearance of reality can bind even the most non-linear set of drawings and unconventional narratives together. What is ultimately important is that the storyboard depicts the direction of movement and that it frames and communicates key events in the film clearly.'

Off-screen space and the illusion of depth
—

'Connected with the concept and the appearance of reality is the establishment of "off-screen space". Off-screen space is what the viewer physically cannot see, but believes exists beyond the limits of the visible frame. An object that is partially seen, for example, extends beyond the parameters of the frame. This can also be achieved through off-screen dialogue between characters, off-screen sound, character reaction and subjects entering and exiting the screen space. The illusion of depth is another space that has to be created and given consideration. The set, scene or background is an integral part of the composition and has to be arranged in a way that will support the theme, main character or subject. The arrangement of materials and "props" can be used to frame the main character, focus attention and indicate both a relationship to the drawn and described environment. It also communicates to the viewer the space has a "textural" depth and is not merely a backdrop for action to take place in.'

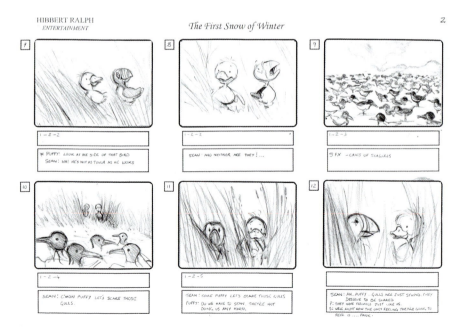

2.12 (pp. 38–43)

Storyboard for *The First Snow of Winter* — Hibbert Ralph

A narrative premise: Here there is a simple example of a 'narrative premise' or the prompt to a 'story event'. Puffy suggests to Sean that they should scatter a flock of gulls. Such prompts introduce and stimulate pictorial action.

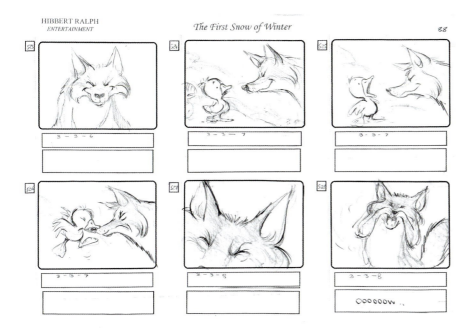

HIBBERT RALPH
ENTERTAINMENT

The First Snow of Winter

88

Visual detail in action sequences:
Storyboards can add a high degree
of visual detail in action sequences
– here Sean bites the fox's nose.
The action and expressions become
vital storytelling ingredients.

Drawing within the space frame

—

'In most cases the picture field will have four
"borders" and these act as the parameters of the
space frame. Images that are introduced should
be essential to the scripted material and content
explored, and be located in response to the limits
of the space within the frame. It is important to
recognise that elements introduced into this "field"
will create, alter and affect the space. If elements
already exist in this space the introduction of new
elements and their subsequent occupancy will
affect the overall composition and they will begin to
assume a spatial relationship. Their occupancy may
create spatial significance and images depicted may
appear to recede or approach pictorially depending
on the overall design. These decisions must be made
in relation to the content of the material and the
purpose of the shot, as these will directly influence
decisions regarding location and prominence of
these elements. The nature of storyboarding allows
for continual revision and this is central to reaching
effective composition.'

Visual difference in sequential drawing

—

'One of the functions of storyboarding is that it can indicate potential problems in pictorial design and sequence order before the project reaches the production stages of the animation. The storyboard may indicate that the drawings do not contain the range of shots necessary to create visual interest. The framing of individual shots may suggest an over-reliance on one fixed viewpoint or that the action depicted takes place principally in the foreground. One approach to discovering the range of images possible in storyboard drawings is to assume that your eye functions as a film/video camera. That it has the facility to track, pan, zoom, use high and low angles to record action and utilise a range of shots and lenses that include long, medium, close-up, extreme close-up and wide-angle camera techniques. Another technique is the use of tonality to direct attention to a given event or subject. Every picture has a range of tone contained within it, levels of brightness alternating with areas of darkness. It is important to constantly remind yourself how the scene is lit and where and how the light falls on the various elements within a shot.'

Using objects to carry the narrative:
The action of a narrative is not always carried by characters, but by objects and environments. This falling stone – itself a version of the traditional 'bouncing ball' cycle most animators practise – drives the 'what happens next?' aspect of the story. Notice too, that the camera pans with the fall of the object, enhancing the movement of the stone and the distance it travels.

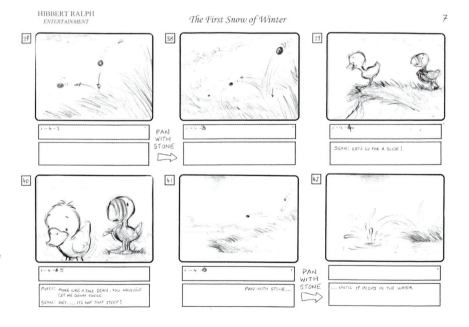

40

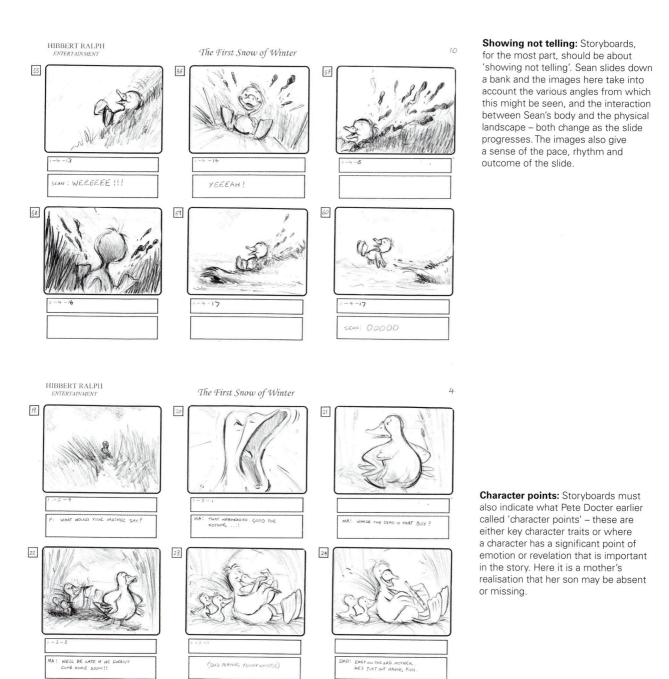

Showing not telling: Storyboards, for the most part, should be about 'showing not telling'. Sean slides down a bank and the images here take into account the various angles from which this might be seen, and the interaction between Sean's body and the physical landscape – both change as the slide progresses. The images also give a sense of the pace, rhythm and outcome of the slide.

Character points: Storyboards must also indicate what Pete Docter earlier called 'character points' – these are either key character traits or where a character has a significant point of emotion or revelation that is important in the story. Here it is a mother's realisation that her son may be absent or missing.

Contextualising narrative points: This is sometimes significant in establishing a specific mood. Here the bird flying, the two figures staring out, the sense of stillness etc., all help to create an atmosphere and a suitable context for Sean's feelings to be expressed.

Diplexcito: 'It is worth noting that effective pictorial design is not the quest for a magical series of symmetrical compositions. The nature of the frame is that it acts as a locating device. If the figure or subject is framed centrally, it may lead to problems with the dynamic operation and symmetrical balance of the image. The "rule of thirds" is a method that may lead to more dynamic compositions, as this involves sectioning the space frame equally into thirds with an invisible grid of horizontal and vertical lines. The intersection of these lines is where the main activity of the composition takes place. This practice allows for the interplay of elements and can create a more dynamic and balanced composition.

'Picture composition is about looking, it is about experimentation, invention and experience. Storyboards allow you to be both experimental and creative in your compositions. It is important to analyse films themselves; the movement within the images, the movement of the camera and how these individual shots are assembled together in editing. It is important that this research includes animation, but also picture design from other disciplines – painting, photography and graphics – to inform your own work.

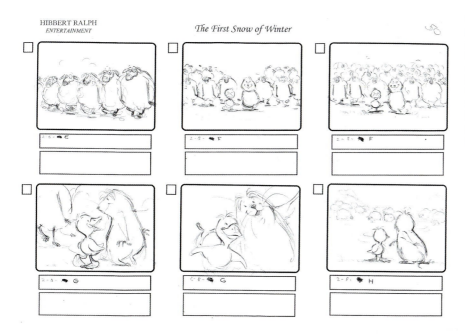

Visual jokes: Storyboards may also illustrate purely visual sequences. One of the best visual jokes in the film is the 'Riverdance' sequence where the main characters are joined by many others in a dance routine, which works as a 'comic event' because as the dance unfolds more and more characters join in, seemingly from nowhere. This is all achieved through the management of the frame.

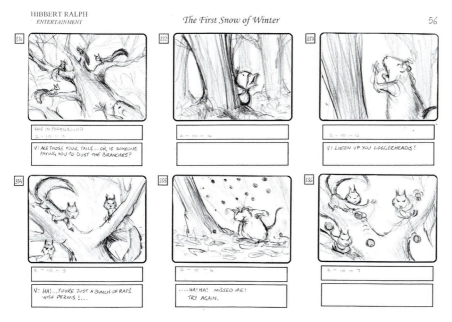

Action sequences: Related to purely visual sequences are action sequences and the visual dynamics that sometimes facilitate conflict and confrontation – the example here is the fight with the squirrels.

Character and Movement

—

Andrew Selby is an award-winning illustrator and a lecturer at Loughborough University, UK. He is committed to the view that character is central to inventive narrative, but equally, characters need to be developed as complex devices in their own right, and all their potential facets and nuances explored, using whatever approach – however unusual – is required.

A series of processes

—

Selby: 'Character development involves a series of processes. Whilst these processes have an order, it should be noted that there is not the perfect recipe to make a successful character. To generalise, a well-conceived character or series of characters will allow the audience to believe and empathise with them. After all, if we as an audience cannot get excited about a character, or share in their joy or pain or fear, we will struggle to believe the story or series of events being portrayed.'

Acute observation

—

Selby says, 'Successful character development starts off with acute observation. It is widely believed that Nick Park's character Gromit the dog is a parody of his own mother. In this particular example, the feat is even more astounding because Gromit has no speech or dialogue with other characters in *The Wrong Trousers* (Aardman Animation, 1993); instead Park uses now famous facial expressions and subtle gestures to illustrate the pet's feelings to the audience.

'As a creatively visual student within a communication medium, being observant is a minimum requirement. You will need a great deal of visually observed material – an animator's sketchbook will typically contain a multitude of drawings, often of the same subject, from different positions. This allows the animator to understand their subject(s), not only in the way the figure moves, but also in its intricacies and individual subtleties. Animator's sketchbooks are an essential reference tool that are used over and over again, recycling imagery by changing features, profiles and adding weight to characters.'

2.13

Creature Comforts — **Nick Park**

Nick Park has become one of Britain's leading animators. *Creature Comforts* (Aardman Animations, 1989), his first Oscar-winning film, features animal characters with the voices of real people talking, offering their views on their own living accommodation and of animals in zoos. The successful combination of the 'right' animal to the voice – here a South American student talking about his experience of England speaking from a languid though highly gestural panther – both creates a winning character and achieves comic effect. This requires close observation and knowledge of human traits and attitudes, and is perhaps best represented in Park's most famous characters, Wallace and Gromit.

Script analysis

—

'Once back in the studio, the animator will analyse the script closely to try and imagine the character as a real-life entity. This will typically involve the animator taking on the perceived persona of that character, human or otherwise, and observing this in a mirror. It will usually involve acting and probably making a fool of yourself in the process! But if you want the character to be truly believable, the first person you have got to convince is yourself.

'How will the character look? What kind of artistic treatment do you intend to visually describe your character? These decisions now need to be pondered. Making the first marks on the paper to try and work these questions out can be daunting. Some students find that working from an unusual starting point helps. Maybe random ink spots on a page create a shape or profile. Maybe a scribble over the sheet results in shapes appearing out of negative spaces, or perhaps standing on a chair dropping objects at random on to the floor. You might want to crop into areas, using a viewfinder, or maybe a digital camera and record your options. Sounds stupid? You've got permission to be stupid. Using your imagination and linking this creatively to your observation is at the very core of your personal vision of the work you produce. It is the very essence of creating an individual, original character.

'As you "adopt" the persona of the character, you need to start recording this information through a series of drawings. Remember that these drawings will never make it to the final cut; they are merely a device to help the animator understand his character. So they can be created in any appropriate medium. Some animators will use graphite sticks to quickly deal with gesture and form of the figure, whilst others will draw with more of a pointed medium.

'Pin the drawings up in your studio. Surround yourself with what you have created. This is the point where the animator can begin to test his character out. For characters that have entirely believable human characteristics, the audience already buy into the character because they are used to seeing the human figure portrayed in this way through photography, television and film.

'The process of development is not a straightforward series of events leading to a memorable character. Repeats of certain stages might need to be covered to further convince you (the animator) and your audience of certain key characteristics of your character. This can initially be frustrating for students who want to get on and shoot the film, but preparation at this stage is the key to success. Be patient! Once satisfied, the most important studies are committed to camera as a series of screen shots creating a basic animatic of the character. These will look like a series of freeze frames. From these still studies, the animator uses the knowledge gained from acute observation and continual drawing of the movement of his character to begin to create a walk cycle, where issues concerning movement of the character(s) will be experimented with and determined.

'Most college students of animation will not work as part of a team when they first encounter the subject of character development. Instead they will be required not only to be the director, but also the character development artist, the sound crew, the storyboard artist and a million things besides. However, it is important for you to see how the process works in a production company as you might be able to develop your skills further by joining and learning along with other creatively minded people.'

THE FIRST SNOW OF WINTER

MODEL SHEETS   SEAN

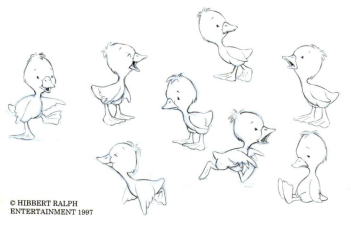

© HIBBERT RALPH
ENTERTAINMENT 1997

THE FIRST SNOW OF WINTER

MODEL SHEETS   SEAN - DETAILS

© HIBBERT RALPH
ENTERTAINMENT 1997

THE FIRST SNOW OF WINTER

MODEL SHEETS   SEAN - HEADS

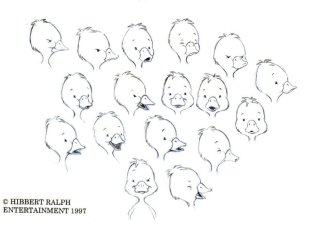

© HIBBERT RALPH
ENTERTAINMENT 1997

2.14

**Model sheets for *The First Snow of Winter* —
Hibbert Ralph**

These model sheets for the main character
Sean indicate his facial expressions and head
movement; his body posture from various
angles; and the 'details' that distinguish his
visual identity.

Bill Plympton, one of the world's most successful animators, offers a perspective from his time as a political cartoonist, stressing the relationship between the possible 'ordinariness' of a cartoon character and the 'exaggeration' of the events he participates in.

Plympton: 'Often character designers say because it is a cartoon, you have got to make a character "goofy"; you have got to give him a big nose and big ears and bulging eyeballs and buck teeth, and I go totally the opposite way; I think that the character should be extremely bland; really normal; sort of nondescript in his characteristics because when something weird happens to him, when he's excited, or when he gets eaten, or something like that, when he freaks out, there is a real contrast. And that's the secret of good animation – the movement between something that is sedate to something that is extreme, and that's what I play off, and that's what I think is important. I think that a good example is still Monty Python because these characters are very straight people – insurance salesmen, accountants, whatever – and then they want to hunt lions, and get drawn into Terry Gilliam's crazy animation.'

2.16
25 Ways to Stop Smoking — **Bill Plympton**

Plympton's signature-style 'average' guy, seen here trying to give up smoking in one of the extreme ways offered up in *25 Ways to Stop Smoking*, demonstrates the juxtaposition between the plain, undemonstrative orthodoxies of the character and the excesses of the things he does, or that happen to him.

2.15
Jiři Trnka's puppet characters in *A Midsummer Night's Dream* (1959) evidence his background in illustration. The animator invests time and effort in a series of engaging observations of the way string puppets can mimic human conditions, drawing on his Eastern European cultural background.

Production Design

—

The Brothers McLeod are illustrator–animator Greg and screenwriter Myles. They are known for their animations created for TV, short film, games and the Web. They have developed, written and directed several TV series, and directed TV commercial campaigns for Skittles, Stena Line and Guinness among others. They are multiple award winning and in 2011 they won a BAFTA for their work with BBC Learning.

'Usually the ideas for a production either come from Myles' script, or it's lots and lots of doodling and painting in sketchbooks which might drive an idea. It's a sort of gut reaction that you get to something that really works.'

2.17

Production designs and stills from *Isle of Spagg* — Brothers McLeod

'Myles and I are both colour blind so colour has a strange relationship with both of us. Sometimes we get comments about purple skies, when I think they're blue, or red foliage when I think they're green, but on the whole it's fine. The use of colour [in our work] has a lot to do with directing you, the viewer, to something we want you to look at.'

McLeod says that it is important for the production designer to bring 'something of themselves' to the designing of the project. Work with people you trust and who share the same sensibility. 'Sometimes clients send us ideas of a design they would like but on the whole hopefully people come to us because they like our style and want something done like it.'

'A lot of what I do is quite intuitive, I'll draw something for a brief and it comes from just sitting with a big sheet of paper and doodling, or drawing straight into the computer. Sometimes a little doodle will trigger an idea, for instance for our *Fuggy* [2005] film it was a drawing I'd done that generated it, and similarly for the *Isle of Spagg* [2011] it was a series of drawings that inspired it. Other times it is the script that inspires the design; with *Phone Home* [2012] it was the script that the visuals sprang from, so it varies from project to project.

'I design a lot of stuff in *very* rough form, so lots and lots of sketches and lots of quick doodles and ideas, and then I'll edit that down before working on the final art work. So very rarely would I work something up to a final art work if we're not going to use it in the final film – usually it's coming out of lots and lots of sketches. As far as editing images is concerned, it's what I like and think works. In the *Isle of Spagg*, for instance, we needed a pub, and the pub came from partly a real pub and partly a made-up pub, and I did quite a few drawings before I got round to the one I wanted.'

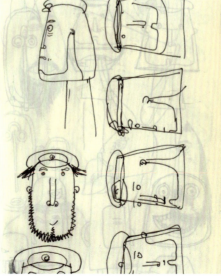

2.18
Examples of designs for characters in *Isle of Spagg*.

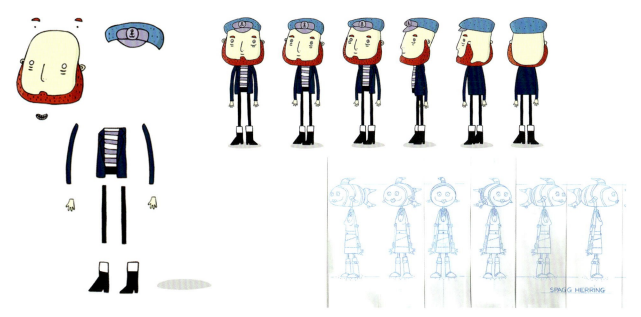

Character Development

—

When developing characters for a film it is essential that they are fit for purpose (see the section Animation for Games in Chapter 12 for a breakdown of developing characters for computer games). Richard Phelan (NFTS, Aardman) talks about the constant refinement of characters in his graduation film *Damned*. For inspiration he says: 'I just looked at loads of stuff; Bill Waterson, old Mickey Mouse, lots of French stuff. Poured it all into a pot and said, right that's the main character. Originally Humphrey [the beaver] was much rounder, it made it very difficult [to animate], he was very fleshy like a little man in a suit.' Eventually Phelan simplified it down to a cube with a little chip off the top, and devised the 'rules' of his animated world within which all the characters worked. For example, 'all the characters were seen three quarter poses, never facing full on or in profile with one eye. They always have two eyes to camera', which gives an aesthetic consistency and coherence.

Phelan advises to think about stance, posture and angle when doing character design. 'Don't use boring poses; think about how the character sees themselves and is seen by others. Think about the way that Buzz Lightyear looks, hands on hips, looking skywards, seen slightly from below. His self-confidence and aspirations are clear just from his stance.'

2.19
These images show the development of the key protagonist in *Damned*, from more realistic to more stylised.

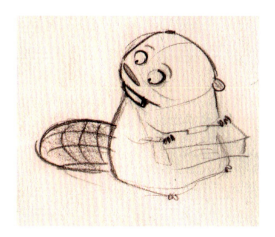

Using the key codes and conventions of cinema

—

Cathal Gaffney has a strong understanding of the relationship between fine art perspectives, cinematic 'genres' and the need to use animation to enhance an 'observational' style. This is cleverly combined in his film, using a variety of highly self-conscious filmic devices.

Gaffney combines his understanding of 'live action' documentary and the traditional ways in which it captures 'actuality' footage' with the graphic freedoms afforded by animation, He uses traditional shots from the documentary style and exaggerates for comic effect through animation.

Gaffney: 'The history of *Give Up Yer Aul Sins* stems back 40 years. A teacher, Margaret Cunningham, brought in an old battered tape recorder to record her seventy pupils in the classrooms of Rutland Street National School, and she told them they were going to be on the wireless. So the little kids – probably beaten in to catechism – were so excited and rattled off the story of John the Baptist. These tapes were ultimately just played back to the pupils as a kind of learning aid for them.

'So later on, Margaret got sick, and the tapes were going to be thrown away, and someone told Father Brian Darcy, and he brought them in to the RTE [Irish Public Service TV and Radio Stations] and had a slot on a radio show and played them. It was an instant success and went on several radio shows, and eventually, EMI Records put them on DC, which sold 80,000 units and the money went to Cunningham's car, and to the school. It went five times platinum in Ireland, and that is pretty big by any standards. It had been around for years. I had never listened to it, and I was driving down to Galway and I heard the story of John the Baptist and I fell about laughing. I bought the CD and contacted EMI, and responded to the Framework Scheme, funded by the RTE and the Arts Council, which gave out £30,000 to make a five-minute short film. We managed to get the funding and I designed the film, and worked with Aland Shannon who did the animation. We worked out the storyboards and scenes, and worked on it between commercial briefs. We did the film in downtime, really. The soundtrack, not matter how many times you heard it, remained fresh.

'The soundtrack itself was actually dreadful – dogs barking, desks falling, the like – so partly as a response to that, and the era it came from, we decided to make it as an animated documentary. We had the cutaway shots and at the end of the film, we have the film itself coming out of the camera, because the soundtrack itself ends abruptly. It was a technique we had to adopt because the story just stops. We animated all the scratches on it and had the microphone coming in and out of the frame. If we had approached that as a computer animation it would have looked dreadful, or if we did some arty style to it, it would not have worked. We just had to do classical animation – 12 drawings per second – to make it work. The response has been overwhelming. Adults and children love it. Adults feel nostalgic about it because you could have such a view today.'

2.22

Give Up Yer Aul Sins – Cathal Gaffney

This traditional establishing shot shows the context in which the story is to take place. Taken from a high and wide perspective, it highlights the way in which the film-maker – in true Hitchcock style – is almost surveying a scene in order to select a story possibility. Here the camper van, driven by the documentary film-makers, begins its approach to the school.

This medium shot focuses on the camper van, but also draws attention to the character of the streets and the people strolling along going about their business.

This medium shot sustains the sense of place, but directs the viewer to where the camper van is heading – the school in the distance.

The camper van moves into close-up. Throughout this introductory sequence, the key questions for the viewer have been: Why are we following this camper van? Who is inside it? Where are we going? The shots have provided the narrative 'hook' at the start of the story, and this is crucial to all successful narrative fiction. Note the background detail of the props supporting the buildings, and the general sense of an old-fashioned and run-down part of the city.

The close-up of the camera sustains the self-reflexive aspect of the piece – this is an animated film about the making of a documentary, so it deliberately calls attention to the film-making process itself.

This 'proscenium'-style medium shot effectively frames the key protagonist – Mary, the little girl on the left – in the context of her classroom and colleagues. There is a general sense of excitement about the presence of the camera and the opportunity to be filmed.

This close-up of Mary in the act of telling the story of John the Baptist defines her character. As in all close-ups, specific character detail and information are revealed. Most importantly, a sense of empathy and engagement with the viewer also takes place in this case.

This close-up again stresses the nature of the character, but also the 'cartoonal' aspect of the film in its design and character performance/movement. The shot also uses the convention of the faded extremities of the frame as a reference to the act of dream, memory or fantasy. This is not the 'real world' where the little girl tells the story, but the world of the imagination, signalled also by the change of time, space, period etc.

This low-angle shot showing both the little girl talking and the camera recording her is a classic shot from the vocabulary of documentary film-making, signalling the presence, but supposed unobtrusiveness, of a 'fly on the wall' crew, who are, of course, in this case, the makers of the animated film.

A traditional medium shot focusing on the conversation between two characters.

A close-up always accentuates 'emotion' and the fundamental relationship the characters have with the audience.

The vitality and affecting expressiveness of the little girl as she gets carried away with telling the story is captured in this exuberant leap.

Here the animation itself becomes important, both in the literal re-enactment of the girl's storytelling – Jesus curing the lepers – and in the facilitation of a visual gag not possible in live action.

This extreme close-up accentuates the physical action in the frame and exaggerates the emotion even more than when held in close-up. Here the blind lady can see again.

The image here supports the perception of the 'lame' as imagined by the little girl, and the apparent 'ease' of the miracle as God enables them to walk again.

Here the medium shot accentuates the comic movement of the character as he celebrates the miracles performed by Jesus.

An important functional use of the medium/close shot to give specific and significant information to the viewer, but here also operating as a gag – a modern party invite for Salome, 'the wicked lady'.

Salome's dance played out not as an erotic fantasy, but as an exaggerated show dance, foregrounding the possibilities of accentuation and exaggeration of the body in animation.

A good example of composition of crowds: John is diminished in status by being placed towards the background, but remains the focus of the scene as he is in the middle at the key point of perspective. The soldiers, though overpowering him as a group, still defer to John – the central protagonist in the story and the key figure of empathy within the image – because of this composition.

Sound

—

While sound design, music and animation can be thought of as separate practices with independent techniques and discourses, it is within the establishment of relationships between these art forms that we begin to recognise contemporary animated film.

Adam Goddard is a Canadian composer, producer and recording artist based in Toronto. His quirky music and varied vocalisations can be heard on broadcasters including Disney Jr. US, Nickelodeon Jr. UK and KidsCBC in Canada. Adam's work has attracted many awards including the Prix Italia and Premios Ondas for his work in experimental audio art with the Canadian Broadcasting Corporation. He currently co-creates and co-produces the children's programme *Big Block Singsong* with his creative partner, director Warren Brown.

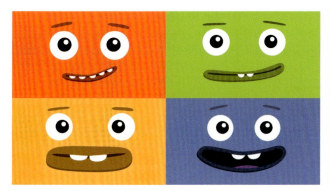

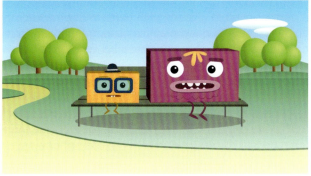

2.23

Big Block Singsong – **Adam Goddard and Warren Brown**

Each episode of this pre-school TV series is based around a song dealing with a particular subject, idea or emotion.

Dope sheet specifics

—

Johnson (cont.): 'Typically, each sheet holds four seconds of screen time. The sheets that are used on projects to be shown at the film speed of 24 frames (exposures) per second have spaces representing 96 frames running down their length. On the other hand, where television is shown at a multiple of 25 frames per second, as in the UK, 100 frames represents four seconds of televised time. Because so much animation is made for television, you are more likely to encounter this type of dope sheet.

'The dope sheets shown here (see pp. 68–73) were designed for duplication on standard A4 photocopier paper and are smaller than industry standard sheets, representing only two seconds of time instead of the usual four. The top of the dope sheet provides spaces for information that typically would only appear on the first camera instruction sheet. The obvious exception is the sheet number, which appears on the top right in each case and is consecutive.

'Reading from the left, the other information provided is the title of the production and episode (if any), the number of the sequence (made up of interrelated scenes), the scene (or shot) number, the name of the animator (and sometimes the assistant as well), the duration of the shot in whole seconds with residual frames, the total frame count, and the length of the shot in feet. This last item relates to film and the way animators were often paid. In one foot of 35 mm film there are 16 frames. If you were making animation drawings to be filmed at two exposures per drawing you would have to produce eight drawings to create a foot of filmed animation. If you were being paid a set rate per foot you would have a fairly clear idea of how productive you would need to be to make a living.'

Preliminary script recording

—

PIXAR director Pete Docter and editor Lee Unkrich note that in the process of the preliminary recording of the script, with additional improvisation by the actors, they can make particular choices about 'performance', which will finally take its place on the 'dope sheet' variants.

Docter: 'So we have all this great material and we have to make all the difficult selections – which line is the funniest, which one do we want to use. In more cases than not we end up cutting performances together, so that what seems on the screen to be "one line" is actually the editors assembling the perfect take.'

Unkrich: 'It is a real luxury for our medium that you do not have in live action because you don't have to "opt" for the performance you have. You can make choices, syllable by syllable sometimes, but if we have done it so seamlessly that the audience doesn't notice, you end up with a really great performance.'[2]

NOTE

2. Quoted in the PIXAR Animation Masterclass, London Film Festival, National Film Theatre, November 2001.

Lip-synching

—

Lip-synching can be problematic for some animators, but basic approaches can sometimes work well.

Plympton: 'The minimal approach to "lip-synch" is all about money and time – four drawings with four different mouth positions. Everything else is exactly the same – I just colour pencilled each one. With those four drawings I think I got two minutes of animation out of it. And the secret is to work with the soundtrack to make sure all the mouth positions work for you. What I do is say the words in front of the mirror – basically I do a slow-motion version of the words like "The secret of li-fe-e" – and find the appropriate mouth positions first. One of the things that I didn't realise, and the famous Warner Bros. animator, Preston Blair told me – I met with him before he died – was that people don't actually close their mouths after they say something. Mouths remain open. So I leave the mouths open for about half a second longer, and it makes it more natural, makes it more real.'

TUTORIAL

Dope sheet basics

—

In traditional drawn, cel animation and stop-motion animation, the 'dope sheet' – essentially the information required to execute the animation in relation to the soundtrack – is crucial to the planning and timing of the work. Here Arril Johnson explains a basic dope sheet, and though with the advent of more and more computer-generated work this is now less used, its principles are still helpful to all aspiring animators in terms of embracing core animation skills.

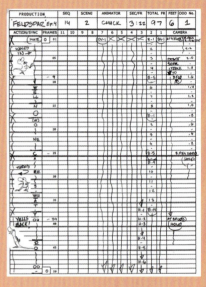

PRODUCTION	SEQ	SCENE	ANIMATOR	SEC/FR	TOTAL FR	FEET	ODD No.
'FELDSPAR' Ep.4	14	2	CHUCK	3:22	97	6	1

Diagram 1

In this case, in order to help with the numbering of the frame count, there are two types of sheets; odd numbered and even numbered. The sheet marked 'ODD No.' shows a frame column starting at '1' (see far right column of Diagram 1) and ending at '50'. The 'EVEN No.' sheet shows frames marked running from '51' to '00'. Put a '1' in the box to the left of '00' and you have an indication of '100' frames. Sheet 1 is odd, sheet 2 is even, sheet 3 would be odd, 4 even, and so on. If you put a '1' next to the '01' at the top of odd sheet 3 it would read frame '101' and at the bottom a '1' next to '50' means frame number '150'. On even-numbered sheet 4, a '1' goes next to '51' and a '2' goes next to '00'. In other words, at the end of sheet 4 you will have reached your 200th frame; eight seconds of animation at 25 frames per second. This is easier than it reads and it does give you control.

So, this is your first exposure, frame one, at the top of dope sheet one.

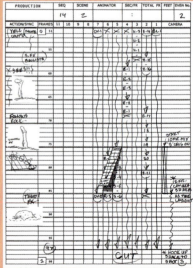

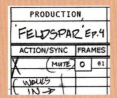

Diagram 2

This is your sample scene's last frame, 97 shortly followed by the last frame on sheet 2, frame 100; four seconds of screen time on these A4-sized dope sheets.

Diagram 4

Thumbnails are simple, expressive drawings of certain key moments in the performance of the action, and on many dope sheets are often less than an inch high. They can help clarify the body language needed in the final animation. Another rough diagram also appears in the action column on the second sheet of the sample doping.

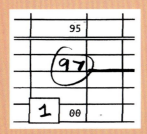

Diagram 3

Almost anyone animating can make use of the information (on the facing page). You need to know how long your scenes (and whole film) will last if you're going to manage the pacing of the film, fill a predetermined broadcasting time slot, or just manage your own time in order to finish a personal film.

The column on the left of the dope sheet, next to the frame count, is often marked 'Action/Sync'. This refers to a description of the action as it unfolds and any specific information about the soundtrack. Something that is equally useful to both graphic and model animators often appears in the action column of dope sheets: thumbnail sketches.

Diagram 5

This describes the trajectory and acceleration of the stone that eventually lands on the character. In addition, it shows the angle of light that determines where the stone's shadow should be as it moves.

The 'X' and '(' symbols in the action column are my personal method of indicating where the main drawings, the keys, and the linking drawings, the in-betweens, occur on the timeline.

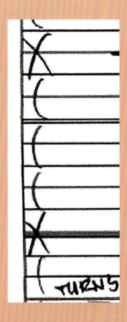

Diagram 6

The 'X' represents a key and the '(' an in-between. In this case, each is photographed or captured for two frames. Called 'animating on twos', this cuts your work in half. When timing the intended animation in order to know where the keys, in-betweens and pauses should occur, I find it useful to make up vocal sound effects that mimic the physical rhythm of the action. That way it is possible to stop flailing around the room as I repeatedly act out the animation and, instead, sit down with the stopwatch and analyse the 'music' of the action.

Next to the action notes in the 'Action/Sync' column is a detailed analysis or breakdown of the soundtrack, which synchronises with the animation.

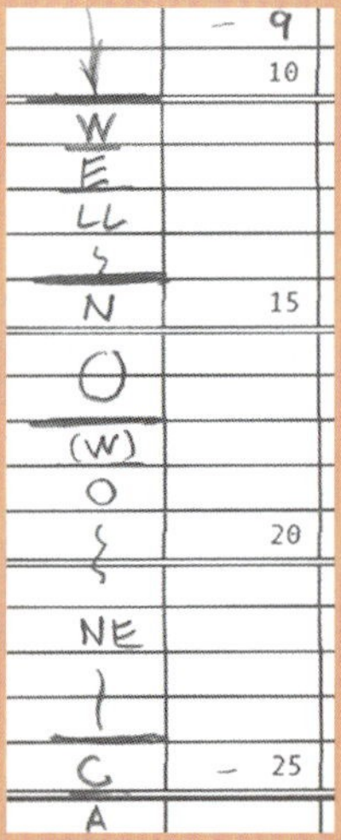

Diagram 7

It could be anything, sometimes music, but in this example it is the pre-recorded voice of the character. In addition to creating a believable performance of the action, the animation must convince the audience that this voice is coming out of the character as the action occurs. It must remain synchronised to the character's lips and be integrated into the total performance. The character's body language, however, usually anticipates the spoken words by several or sometimes more than several frames. First of all, most people think before they speak and the gestures of the face and whole body reflect these thoughts and feelings. Secondly, if the character assumes a new position just as an important word is being spoken, the audience might be distracted enough by the visuals to miss the vocal emphasis on that word. The picture and sound need to integrate, not compete, and the character's body language needs to create the illusion of thought.

To the right of the 'Action/Sync' and 'Frames' columns are the numbered columns indicating different levels of artwork. These are only applicable to drawn animation, whether it is scanned into a computer and composited or traced on to clear cels and photographed.

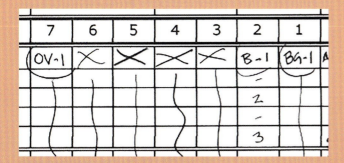

Diagram 8

Number 1 is the lowest level and, in this case, is reserved for the background, BG-1. Here level 7 is used for OV-1, an overlay of some scenic element that exists above (in front of) all other artwork.

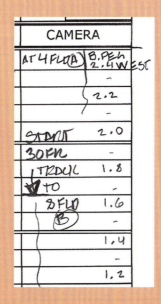

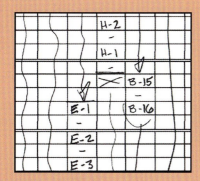

Diagram 9

As the shot progresses, additional artwork appears on various levels with prefixes indicating the nature of the numbered drawings or cels; 'E' for eyes, 'H' for head, 'B' for body, and sometimes a large 'X' indicating a designated level, which currently has a blank cel doped because no artwork is required on that level yet.

Diagram 10

The 'camera' column shows any moves planned for the artwork or camera, as well as any transitional or special effects. In this case, the shot starts at 4 field 'A' with the camera showing a specific portion of the artwork four inches wide. The bottom pegs are indicated as starting at 2.4 inches west (left) of their normal zero position and immediately panning east (right) at a rate of .2 inches every two frames. On the ninth frame of this shot the camera has to start recomposing the picture so that it will end up cropping the artwork at 8 field 'B' at a specific moment in the action 30 frames (one second and five frames) later. Further down the camera column is an instruction in the camera column to 'Start 10 frame mix "S" cels on'.

Technique

The choice of technique for an animator is fundamentally related to key skills, artistic intentions and practical considerations. For some, this is straightforward – traditional drawn/cel animation; stop-motion animation using clay, puppets or objects; or computer-generated animation, using a variety of software applications. Increasingly the flexibility that mastering digital software provides allows the animator to use compositing and mixed media in their work.

Compositing is the process of bringing together disparate elements to create a whole on the screen. This can be done to look photorealistically seamless (this type of compositing moves into the realm of visual effects, VFX), or it can be used creatively to construct a world of the animator's imagination. Although now we generally refer to digital compositing when we use the term, the basics of the process have been used for years by animators. Georges Méliès was a pioneer in the field. In contemporary animation a combination of digital and analogue compositing is likely to be used.

Compositing
—

ArthurCox animation studio has always used compositing in an inventive way, from the use of hand-made knitting in *Don't Let It All Unravel* to the digital compositing of *A Pig's Tail*. Director Sarah Cox describes her early interest in this way of working.

Cox: 'I have always used mixed media – I think it is because when I first got into animation at college it was from an interest in experimental cinema rather than the traditional route. I loved the work of Len Lye, Stan Brakhage, Norman Maclaren and most of all Robert Breer. I felt very strongly that different materials and media are better at expressing different things. With the Boots No 7 ads that we did the agency were very keen that what they were selling was colour. We used the shadows of a children's mobile – we filmed the shadows through gauzes and trace and angled planes to create a slipping, glimpsing feel that would have been unobtainable through traditional animation.'

The *Liar's Autobiography* sequences made by ArthurCox were directed by George Sander Jackson and Matthew Walker. George's oil-on-glass sequences were created directly under camera to create the nightmarish sensation of recovering from alcoholism: 'It was all shot as if POV [point of view] and the animation was filmed under camera in several layers – we simply used [digital] compositing to put the layers

3.1
An early example of compositing: *L'homme à la tête de caoutchouc* (The Man with the Rubber Head), 1901 – Georges Méliès.

together, it made the under camera animation simpler. We also had to negotiate compositing for 3D cinema and that took a few stages to get right – but we think that these sequences are the first ever oil on glass 3D [stereoscopic] animations.

'*Don't Let it All Unravel* was process led – the brief was 'Save Ourselves' within an environmental context and I thought about how quick it is to unravel something (like a jumper) that would have been so painstakingly slow to put together – creation being a slower and more difficult thing than destruction. So I created knitted endangered species of plants and animals and unravelled them frame by frame. I also made a knitted globe and unravelled the ice caps – we filmed each element separately in the studio and then composited together with a little toy plane that circled the globe. We gave it a trail that looked like a piece of wool so it looked like the plane was unravelling the globe.'

Sarah thinks that compositing is entirely part of the process in contemporary animation, it is 'completely intrinsic – I can't think of a production we have done in the last five years that doesn't entail some basic compositing'.

Currently Sarah is directing a pre-school series for Disney called *Nina Needs to Go.* 'It is quite traditional Flash animation with lots of background characters and detail; we use compositing to bring it all together and to create a few SFX – there is a lot of water in each episode as it is about a little girl who suddenly needs to get to the bathroom. We have also sneaked a few CG elements in there and we have composited them in quite carefully so they blend in with the Flash elements.

'We just finished a community production for Aardman and the Historic Royal Palaces where we worked with eight-year-old children from a school in Tower Hamlets to make a film about Anne Boleyn's Coronation. The children all drew individual characters, backgrounds and props and we animated them and brought them all together in the composite – for this project we were making a piece to go in the igloo which is a 360 projection – so our ultimate aspect ratio was 9200 x 1080 which is a really long strip and as it was viewed in the round the two ends had to join up. As a project compositing was therefore an essential and rather technical part of the process.'

Mixed-media animation: *Dad's Dead*

—

The multi award-winning *Dad's Dead*, made by Chris Shepherd, is an excellent example of a mixed-media animation, and one that also points out the relationship between live action and animation.

Shepherd had returned to his roots in Liverpool and discovered that the Eileen Craven Primary School, which he had attended as a boy, had been vandalised and burnt out. The destruction of the school prompted Shepherd to consider his memories of school and the formative context that it had been, and his mixed feelings about its influence. He was keen to find an approach to the subject matter where the animation could facilitate a film taking place in someone's head, and that the assumed 'innocence' of animation could be contradicted by dark, fantastic and subversive things taking place in an ordinary, run-down, derelict, everyday terrain.

Having completed a provisional shooting script, Shepherd cast 'real scouser', Ian Hart, for his voice-over, and shot live-action material in six separate shoots over seven months, attempting to 'build the film up like a painting', creating an animatic alongside the live-action material that would suggest how the animation would interact and counterpoint the dramatic action featuring Johnno, the dysfunctional youth at the heart of the story. Shepherd wanted to make a film that people might find disturbing and perhaps not like, but ironically, the film has been embraced as a challenging portrayal of the way that 'nostalgia' is easily triggered, but may not be comforting if remembered as it actually was.

Shepherd encourages the view that the only effective way to make a film is to be 'true to yourself' and to explore your own world carefully for the inspiration it can bring, stressing 'what can be boring to you can be interesting to someone else if presented as an engaging story'. This chimes with the view of John Lasseter – the director of *Toy Story* (Pixar/Walt Disney Pictures, 1995) and *Toy Story 2* (1999) – that research and observation are absolutely vital because 'nothing is more interesting or rich than what is actually there, once you look at it with a truthful, but creative eye'. Shepherd's story, the memory of the relationship between the narrator and Johnno, recalled in a range of challenging vignettes – destroying an ice cream van; spray-painting dead pigeons and torturing animals; Johnno lying about his father's death; Johnno's abuse of a blind man he supposedly cares for; and the torching of a run-down flat – also explores the received associations of mediated imagery.

Shepherd is highly successful in offering a commentary on the uses and meanings of animated imagery while using animation to reinvent controversial documentary-style domestic drama.

3.2

Dad's Dead – **Chris Shepherd and Maria Manton**

The innocuous child-friendly images on the side of the ice cream van are animated to echo Johnno's brutality. The sharp-toothed figure beats up the rabbits. Simultaneously, the innocence of animated animal characters is subverted and revised.

This theme continues throughout the film as an elephant, which is animated dancing on a child's birthday card and inevitably suggests Disney's Dumbo, is later hanged as Johnno torches a flat. All innocence has been completely lost and the image works as a metaphor for a personal, social and cultural world in decline.

The narrator, when fleeing from Johnno's house, finds a Ladybird book – one actually found on the ground at the location – and when animated, this initially embodies happy memories with 'Auntie May', and the apparent stability of a family structure. The images for the Ladybird books were drawn by Martin Aitchison and John Berry, and clearly represent a safe, middle-class, trouble-free England, which was clearly not the experience of Johnno and his kind. The film represents his disempowerment by animating obscene graffiti on the Ladybird images.

The translucent, almost supernatural figure of Johnno as he throws stones at ducks on a pond; one animated to show a fleeing 'cartoonal' duck and to once more point out the difference between fantasy and reality; innocence and experience; life and death.

3.3

Production still from *LearnDirect Bus* – DFGW/COI/Maria Manton/Chris Shepherd

Ironically, this graffiti style prompted a commission from LearnDirect to make a public information film based on the 'doodling' readers do on newspapers when considering an advertisement.

3.4

Stills from *Dad's Dead* – Chris Shepherd and Maria Manton

Shepherd distorts Johnno's face at certain moments to show the psychological and emotional complexity of the character as he plays out his conscious frustration, anger and brutality. It was Shepherd's desire to create a 'live-action Francis Bacon' painting with such imagery.

3.5

Stills from *Loetzinn* – Aaron Bradbury and Chris Gooch

Bradbury and Gooch's *Loetzinn* is set in a barren and hostile landscape. The two main characters are two old mechanical toy boats that happen to cross each other's path as they travel endlessly across the vast ocean. Their un-oiled joints squeak and creak as they struggle towards each other. Their pathetic efforts to destroy each other are more than futile. The film operates in a 'tragi-comic' style in the sense that the amusement arises from the ludicrous and inept nature of their struggle. Animation for the motion of the boats was achieved by using a mix of dynamics solutions and key-framing. By animating in this way there is in some ways a relationship to puppetry, again giving a sense of the traditional even when using digital applications.

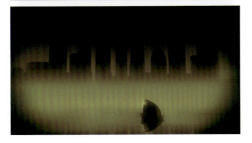

The Animator as Interpreter

Inventing scenarios, writing scripts and creating funny material are all particular interpretative and creative skills needed by the animator. What solutions are dramatically viable, offer comic situations and are particularly suited to animation?

Script and Scenario

Animation practitioners approach the execution of what they wish to create in a variety of ways. Some receive a script and interpret it; others write their own. In either case, it is crucial for the writer to engage with the distinctive 'language' of animation, the core principles of scriptwriting and, often, the issues that inform the creation of an original and particular 'world' that only animation can facilitate. All these issues are considered here.

The distinctive language of animation can be summarised as follows – any one element or more might be intrinsic to an individual approach:

■ *Metamorphosis*: the ability to facilitate the change from one form into another without edit.

■ *Condensation*: the maximum degree of suggestion in the minimum amount of imagery.

■ *Anthropomorphism*: the imposition of human traits on animals, objects and environments.

■ *Fabrication*: the physical and material creation of imaginary figures and spaces.

■ *Penetration*: the visualisation of unimaginable psychological/physical/technical 'interiors'.

■ *Symbolic association*: the use of abstract visual signs and their related meanings.

Having considered the 'language' of animation and how it might be applied to a potential work, developing a script is essential, especially in 'narrative'-driven works. Award-winning animation scriptwriter Alan Gilbey of Peafur Productions suggests the following when approaching the task.

Gilbey: 'The tough truth is that if you wish to make movies an audience will watch to the end you must win, hold and deserve their attention. Your holy creative duties are:

■ to intrigue your audience;

■ to take them on a journey that exceeds their expectations;

■ to leave them somewhere that made their trip worthwhile.'

There are many books about screenwriting and most will tell you the same things: the orthodox theories of film structure. These are not the only ways to make movies, but they are very effective. Any rule of writing can be broken with great success (Belleville Rendez-vous, Tarantino and the Coen brothers all appear to go their own way), but if you break rules without understanding them first, you stand a very good chance of screwing up.

4.1

Stills from *64 Zoo Lane* – John Grace and An Vrombaut

The highly specific world created by Grace and Vrombaut achieves a consistency both in the design and the narrative format (see the section Creative Considerations on p. 85).

64 Zoo Lane
© COPYRIGHT ZOO LANE PRODUCTION 1996

The Story of Zed the Zebra.

CAST

1 Zoo   Lucy
          Georgina the Giraffe
          Giggles and Tickles
          Nelson the Elephant
          Molly the Hippo
          Snipsnip Bird

2 Story   (narrated by the Snipsnip Bird)
          Zed the Zebra
          Ronald the Rhino
          Nelson the Elephant
          Herbert the Warthog
          Georgina the Giraffe
          Nathalie the Antelope
          Snipsnip Bird

--- page 1

64 Zoo Lane

The Story of Zed the Zebra.

1. EXT. ZOO -NIGHT
Lucy slides down Georgina's neck into the Zoo.
When she's landed she ignores the animals and instead
starts to do exercises.

          1. LUCY (touching her toes)
One Two ! One Two!

          2. MOLLY
Lucy, what are you doing?

          3. LUCY
Can't you see? I'm doing exercises.
(Bends sideways)
One Two! One Two!

Lucy runs round Nelson.

          4. LUCY (while running)
I have to get ready for the race tomorrow.

          5. GEORGINA
What race?

          6. LUCY (impatiently)
The potato sack race at school of course.

          7. GIGGLES AND TICKLES (excitedly)
Faster Lucy! Faster!

Lucy keeps on running.
Suddenly Nelson's trunk picks her up.

          8. NELSON
Hey hey hey hey! Wait a moment!

          9. LUCY(protests)
Put me down. I have to practice for the race!

          10. NELSON
Aren't you taking this all a bit too
seriously, Lucy?

          11. LUCY
But I want to win!

          12. MOLLY
We all want to win. But you can't always win.
Sometimes you win and sometimes you lose. . .

          13. SNIPSNIP BIRD (off screen)

--- page 2

. . . but the most important thing
is to have fun!

The SnipSnip Bird lands in the Zoo next to Lucy.

          14. LUCY
You're the Snipsnip Bird, aren't you?

          15. Snipsnip Bird
That's right. And I know all about races!
Let me tell you a story . . .

Nelson shapes his trunk like a swing and Lucy sits down .

          16. Snipsnip Bird
. . . about Zed the Zebra.

2. EXT. AFRICAN SAVANNAH WATER HOLE - DAY
CUT to empty savannah. Grass curtain opens.
Suddenly a black and white blur whizzes past from left to
right. Then it whizzes past from right to left. Then it
stops. It's a zebra.

          17. SNIPSNIP BIRD (V/O)
Zed the Zebra was fast. . .very fast!.
He was the FASTEST RUNNER
in all of Africa.

Zed looks at his own reflection in the water hole and
smiles.

          18. ZED
Just look at those Go Faster Stripes!
I'm so cool!

Suddenly an elephant's trunk slams down in the water hole
spoiling Zed's reflection and slurping up all the water.
It's Nelson the Elephant. Zed looks annoyed.

          19. ZED (has an idea)
Hey Nelson, you're a SLOW runner, aren't you?

          20. NELSON
Slow . . .me? I wouldn't say I was slow.
(Thinks)
In fact I can run quite fast. . .

          21. ZED
. . .for an elephant! Haha!
But you can't run as fast as me !

          22. NELSON (annoyed with Zed)
Says who?

--- page 3

4.2

Script pages from *64 Zoo Lane* – John Grace and An Vrombaut

An example of a traditional approach to script in an episodic children's
animation series.

Creative Considerations

—

It is important to think about how your visual and textual pre-production work relates to a wider scheme of issues with regard to a potential film:

■ the need to create a specific 'world' defined and limited by its own terms and conditions;

■ the consideration of the relationship between narrative and aesthetic requirements, and the economy of the chosen technique;

■ the relationship between character and story events, and the specific elements that will be animated;

■ the imperative of the soundtrack in the determination of the imagery and the timing of the animated elements;

■ the realisation of the performance of character action implied in the script and mediated through voice artists and animators.

An Vrombaut and John Grace created a highly specific world for the popular children's series *64 Zoo Lane*, which had clear instructions about its characters, plot, structure, language and humour, as well as the following dos and don'ts:

■ Animals can move freely within one continent, but cannot travel to other continents.

■ Stick to native animals (no dromedaries in Australia or penguins in the North Pole).

■ If a character appears in a story set in one continent, it cannot appear in a story set in a different continent.

■ No humans, human footprints, litter left behind by humans or any other signs of human civilisation.

■ Props should always be made of materials the animals can find in their natural environment. Keep props simple (no machines).

■ Don't set a story within a story.

■ Avoid flashbacks.

This gave a consistency to the piece that children could engage with and soon grasp the parameters of.

Script Development

—

Alan Gilbey has co-developed shows with Aardman Animation, Cosgrove Hall Films, the Disney Channel, Universal Pictures and Fox. He also created and wrote *Aaagh! It's the Mr Hell Show* and *Bounty Hamster*. He has presented highly entertaining workshops on script development. Here are some of the key points he stresses to animators eager to write better material:

Show don't tell
In every book this is rule number one, yet it's one of the hardest to master. Always strive for the most visual ways to tell your story. Let your pictures do the talking and save the talking for things that pictures can't do. When you add words make sure they make a real difference to what we're seeing. If you removed the words from your pictures (or the pictures from your words) and the film still made the same sense then something has gone wrong.

Characters are important
An audience loves characters who intrigue or enchant them. They might be Bart Simpson. They might be an anglepoise lamp. They might be a cute mouse or a reprehensible monster, but if the viewer feels a degree of empathy for them, they will stay the course because they like the things that happen when that character is around.

If you are creating a new character, find out a lot about them before you start writing.

Beware the stock cast of characters you have in your head. They've been put there by a lifetime's exposure to other people's stories and it's easy to repeat too accurately something we've all seen before. Often the best new characters are a blend of something a little familiar (the stoic, silent suffering of Buster Keaton) and something from left field (a dog). Put those together and you get Gromit.

What is your script about?

I don't mean 'what is the story?' That's just the surface. What is it really about? The theme? What's the secret objective of the tale you are telling?

Is *Buffy the Vampire Slayer* about vampires? No, it's about the pains of growing up, using monsters as metaphors. If you have an idea for a story, but no idea of what it is really about, you have a truck but no cargo. Think about something you really want to say, then make your story serve that higher purpose.

Before you start a script answer these questions:

- What does your film seem to be about?
- What is it *really* about?
- What do you want to make your viewers feel?

Your film may not reach any firm conclusions, but it does need a sense of closure or it won't satisfy. It'll just stop. A good ending is the natural, but entirely unpredictable result of all that has gone before. It is your ultimate weapon for leaving the audience in the state you want to leave them – be it laughing, crying or arguing about what you meant.

Three-act structure

There are many ways to hold an audience, but the oldest and most well known is the three-act structure:

Situation
Welcome to my world. I'm going to make you wonder what happens next.

Complication
Ooh! I bet you didn't see that coming. My characters are sent on a journey and no one knows where it will lead them.

Resolution
Blimey, I didn't expect them to end up here!

I believe many scripts go wrong because they only have two acts: the initial idea and its development. Reaching for the third act – the surprising, the less obvious, the twist in the tale – is what will make your film unique. So …

- Draw a flow chart of your film – with three boxes.
- Then scribble out your story so it divides into them.
- If the divisions feel slight or forced, do some more thinking. Is there more that could happen? Is the story really over or is there somewhere else you could go that would bring fresh perspectives to your theme?

B-plots

In a visual medium a single idea can be put over pretty quickly, so you'll need more than a single idea to stop your audience thinking about popcorn.

B-plots can do this. They are miniature three-act tales that weave around your major story and may concern a supporting character. They usually conclude before the main tale does and often reflect another aspect of your secret objective. Or not. Sometimes they are just the comic relief. But, profound or preposterous, they make a film richer.

Riffs and rhythms

Riffs and rhythms can also make films richer. Think of a film as a piece of music. Verse and chorus pace a song and the best songs usually have more than one hook:

- If there is an incidental character, bring them back later, then later still. If they eventually change the course of the main story in some way, all the better.
- Give minor characters teeny three-act stories of their own, even if they're just the cat on the mat in the corner of the room (part of the success of *Creature Comforts*).

■ If a train passes a window, keep the train passing the window at regular intervals. Then let the train passing somehow move your plot forward (at first it was there to show that your characters lived in poor housing, but later someone misses an important part of a conversation because of the noise it makes).

Go back to your flow chart and scribble out some parallel sets of boxes.

Preparing to script

Got everything sorted? Know what your film's about? Good. Next do the following:

■ Write a two- or three-page synopsis of your story with a paragraph for each scene.

■ Write a one-page synopsis with a paragraph for each act.

■ Write a single paragraph for the back of the video box. Make us want to rent your movie.

■ Write a one-line teaser for the poster.

Then go back and rewrite your long synopsis. Does it achieve the aims you set yourself when you did the 'What is your script about?' exercise above (see p. 86)? If it doesn't, rewrite it so it does, THEN start on your script.

Cut, cut, cut and cut again!

As you may have gathered by now, writing really is the act of rewriting. Scripts tend to get better the more you go over them.

Having read a lot of scripts and watched a lot of student films, I can confidently state that:

■ many are far too long;

■ few knew when to stop;

■ most would benefit from harsh, critical cutting.

So be brutal – too brutal – with your cutting. If you want a pacy film, start your scenes late and end them early. Hit the road running and let your audience catch up. If I told you to cut 3 minutes from a 15-minute script, then a week later said you could put the cut scenes back in again, I'm willing to bet good money you'd decline! Comparing the two drafts, you will see that in screenwriting less really is more.

4.3

Sientje – Christa Moesker

Christa Moesker, a graduate of the Netherlands Institute of Animated Film, created *Sientje*. A little girl gets very upset after a quarrel with her parents and gets rid of her frustration through a series of incidents, until peace is restored with her mother.

The film was awarded the prize for Best Short Film 1997 at the Netherlands Film Festival 1997, and at the Festival International du Film d'Animation Annecy 1998 the film was awarded two prizes: Prize for the Best First Film and a Special Mention of the FIPRESCI (The International Federation of Film Critics) Jury. It was also Best Film in the category 30 seconds–6 minutes at the 13th World Festival of Animated Films Zagreb 1998, later becoming a series on Dutch television.

Animated Gags and Comic Events

—

A high number of animated films aspire to be funny. The American cartoonal tradition effectively established the 'gag' as the lingua franca of the animation vocabulary, and much can be learned from simply watching the sight gags in Disney's *Silly Symphonies* or the work of Chuck Jones, Tex Avery and Bob Clampett at Warner Bros. Theories written on comedy argue that there are only a limited number of gags – between four and seven, depending on who you believe – and all else is merely variation or dressing on these core comic structures. The following suggested 'gag' structures are particularly suited to visual humour:

- Misdirection and juxtaposition
- Illogical logic
- Dramatic irony
- Puns and parody
- Exaggeration and understatement
- Repetition

Misdirection and juxtaposition

—

Most comedy is about undermining expectations. Establish one idea or principle, which has a predictable outcome, and then deliberately misdirect the audience to an unexpected conclusion. This is usually done by linking or juxtaposing two unlikely ideas where the incongruity or mismatching of the two ideas creates the joke. John Kricfalusi's *Son of Stimpy* controversially mixes the two ideas of Stimpy's lost 'fart-child' – itself a bizarre incongruity – with the story of Christ.

Illogical logic

Most animation uses its distinctive language of expression to create worlds with their own codes and conventions, however surreal or apparently 'illogical' these principles are, but this is especially important in comic scenarios, where a particular distortion of everyday logic can create jokes. As with misdirection and juxtaposition, this might also resolve itself with a revelation – perhaps a pertinent observation of something that supposedly might or should remain unsaid. Simply telling the truth about a situation is sometimes the most 'illogical logic' of all. Bill Plympton's *I Married a Strange Person* (Universal Studios, 1997) sets up the narrative premise that Grant, the hero, has a satellite-induced boil, which enables him to literally enact his every thought or desire – suddenly his girlfriend's breasts enlarge to take over the house, during sex, or are twisted into a variety of balloon animals!

Dramatic irony

—

This is an important device in any narrative, but is especially useful in comedy. Simply, it is concerned with giving the audience more information about a situation than the characters themselves have. This can often be the prelude to 'bad' things happening to characters, which might result in their humiliation, and that we are permitted to laugh at, rather than have sympathy for. Simple definition: it is 'humour' when it is happening to 'them'; it is 'horror' when it is happening to 'you'. Pure 'irony', of course, is merely saying or implying the opposite of what is meant, knowingly. Effectively, the joke is coming out of the viewer or listener's recognition of the subtext of what is being said. This is essentially the premise of Matt Groening's work in *The Simpsons*, where both Homer and Bart are unknowingly playing out their own limitations, ineptitudes and shortfalls with complete self-belief, unaware that they create social disruption and cultural mayhem. The series itself, though, is wholly self-conscious about the way it parodies American sit-com and exposes social hypocrisy and double standards in society at large. Consequently, its comedy works on a number of levels.

Puns and parody
—

Visual puns play on the possible double meaning in certain kinds of images. Verbal puns play on the double meaning in words. Some images 'substitute' for others and create an amusing juxtaposition or discontinuity; some words 'redirect' the suggested meaning of one interpretation of the word onto another possible level of meaning – sometimes, for example, creating 'innuendo'. Graphic and verbal puns often underpin cliché and stereotype – which, while vilified in much creative expression, is extremely useful in comedy as a shortcut to an immediate and accessible comic possibility. Parody follows on directly from this, in that an existing and well-known person or popular work of art is exaggerated, exploited or critiqued in an act of what might be called 'excessive' reproduction in animation; this is largely in the act of caricature, and is often for political or subversive purposes. Right from the earliest animation, the graphic pun was an important comic device. Felix the Cat uses his tail as a range of objects; castle turrets become ice cream cones etc. The parody, too, was often the best way in which the Warner Bros.'s cartoonists could send up the aesthetic and ideological sensibilities of Disney cartoons, mocking Disney's aspirations to art and culture, or sending up its 'tweeness' and sentimentality.

Exaggeration and understatement
—

Presenting something in an overstated and extreme fashion can successfully draw the humour from a situation. Similarly, the understated or deadpan can also draw the comedy into relief. Excess can often lead to physical or emotional 'cruelty' in comedy, and often needs a 'victim' figure who can be insulted and abused. The main aspect of exaggeration, though, is its flouting of convention, routine and conformity. By 'breaking the rules' of social and cultural representation in a context that signals this is for 'humorous' and not 'harmful' ends, the joke can be successful – but there is arguably sometimes a fine line between the two. Most animated cartoons thrive on a tension between excess and subtlety, but the concept is perhaps best epitomised by Marv Newland's *Bambi Meets Godzilla* in which Disney's Bambi is unceremoniously crushed by the massive foot of Godzilla; end of cartoon. Excessive yet understated, but full of symbolic and metaphorical meaning.

Repetition
—

Repeating something often enough, and in the most surprising contexts, can have the effect of becoming funny. Most catchphrases work in this way, even if they don't seem to intrinsically be 'a joke' in their own right. Similarly, a repeating visual idea or situation can inspire a comic context. Sometimes, for example, in the case of Chuck Jones's Roadrunner cartoons, these repetitions become the minimalist conventions for the maximum of narrative and comic invention.

4.4

Stills from *Monkey Dust* – Steve May

These are Ivan Dobsky and Mr Hoppy, two of the eccentric characters from *Monkey Dust*, which looks at the dark underbelly of British culture, breaking every taboo and critiquing amoral contemporary lifestyles.

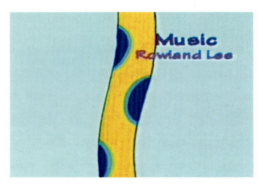

4.5

Screengrabs from the opening sequence of *64 Zoo Lane*

John Grace and An Vrombaut's humour for children is often based on simple distortions of the physical realities they are beginning to understand and embrace. This extended neck of a giraffe simultaneously refers to the 'truth' of the long neck, but at the same time plays with the idea.

4.6

Still from *Creature Comforts* – Nick Park

Much of the humour of *Creature Comforts* comes from the juxtaposition of what is being said with the type of creature chosen to say it, together with the background slapstick gags that accompany the 'interview' with the animal.

The Animator as Performer

Whether working through the pencil, a puppet or pixels, the need to express thought, emotion and action is fundamental to effective animated sequences, and while many voice artists are given credit for the performances in animated films – particularly so that 'stars' can sell animated features – it is the animator who creates the performance of the character through visual means.

Many of the performance issues in relation to animation are intrinsically related to the casting of the voices. Getting this right can enhance the character considerably. John Lasseter and Pete Docter of PIXAR commented on this in their PIXAR Animation Masterclass at the London Film Festival, 2001.

Lasseter: 'The casting of the actors is something we are considering as we are developing the storyboard. We cast for not how big a star they are, but how good an actor they are – how well their natural voice fits in with the character's persona that we are trying to put across. We also hope to get actors who are quite good at ad-libbing. Working on a feature that takes four years to make is like telling the same joke every week for that time; it gets awfully old. We try to look for spontaneity as much as we can.'

Docter: 'What is great about people who can improvise well is that they don't just shoot off and go somewhere else with the material, they stay true to the subject matter that you are trying to put across. They put it into words that are much more natural and believable, without completely going off script. The spontaneity is so valuable.'

Lasseter: 'In casting an actor, we oftentimes take a line of dialogue from a movie or a TV show that they have been in, take away the picture, and put in a drawing or image of the character that we are interested in them playing, and it is remarkable because sometimes when you take away the physical image of these really great actors there is something really lacking – it is flatter than you would expect – but other times it really comes alive with just that voice, and we go with those actors. The next stage is animation. We have the actors' voices. We have the layout. As directors we will first talk to the animators from the standpoint of acting. What is the subtext? We do talk to them also about the practicalities of moving a character from one place to another, but we don't tell them how to do it. Sometimes the animator has a problem about how a character is going to do a certain thing. So the animators will use a video and they will act things out. We have a room that is all mirrors and they will act things out. Even though we are creating fantasy worlds we want to make it believable.'

5.1

Still of Gollum from *The Lord of the Rings* – Peter Jackson

The universally acknowledged 'Gollum' from the *Lord of the Rings* (Universal Studios, 2001–2003) trilogy is a combination of a motion captured performance by Andy Serkis, and an extraordinarily nuanced use of computer-generated animation. Audiences forget that they are watching a CGI character – in a way, for example, that they don't with Jar Jar Binks in *Star Wars* – because of the capacity for Gollum to think, feel and express his tragic contradictions.

5.2

Still from *The Iron Giant* – Brad Bird

Director Brad Bird has suggested that the art of character animation is like 'catching lightning in a bottle one volt at a time', because the animator must work on brief seconds of complex personal exchange over a long period of time; time which passes in live action, literally at the moment of its execution. This attention to detail is reflected in the relationship between the boy and the iron giant in Bird's adaptation of Ted Hughes's poetic narrative.

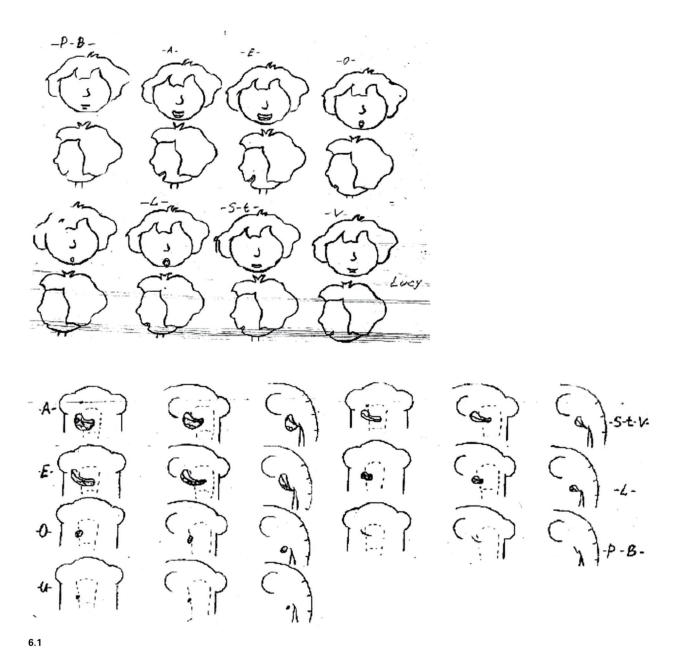

6.1

Sketches for lip-synching – Animation Workshop

Animation Workshop, created by John Grace, Andy Chong and Brian Larkins, demonstrates a number of the core skills in traditional 2D animation, and shows, for example, aspects of 'lip-synching' that in themselves might be related to the ways in which a scene is edited.

and ends at the end there's a good chance that you can cheat the synch – it's always worth a try!

'Ultimately body language may be more critical in maintaining the illusion of synch than the slavish matching of mouth shapes. I was cutting a musical sequence some years ago and it became apparent that whilst the characters' mouths were in perfect synch, their gestures, foot taps and hand movements were somewhat off the beat. We found that if we slipped the synch so that the body movements hit the beats, then nobody queried the lip-synch.

'A small note about lip-synch: most animation manuals give examples of consonant and vowel mouth shapes showing the "plosives" (P, B) as closed mouth-shapes. The truth is the actual sound of a P or B is emitted on the first, small, opening of the mouth – that's when the pressure, built-up whilst the lips are pressed together, is released. Try it yourself! I suspect that this is at the root of the myth, rife in animation circles, that synch looks better if the sound is two frames late – what's really happening is that the sound is being repositioned to where it should have been in the first place!

'Every cut should have a positive motivation stemming from the needs of the story. It is not unknown in animation for seemingly arbitrary cuts to appear because shot A ran into difficulties or it was physically impossible to show a particular piece of action. Obviously these situations do occur and have to be addressed – the trick is to make the solution appear to be dramatically motivated; whatever you cut to should enhance the audience's understanding of the scene otherwise it will feel let down and your momentum will have been lost.

'To illustrate, consider this example: a character is running along and jumps into his waiting vehicle; we're talking puppet animation here so jumping is difficult or perhaps even impossible to execute. The director suggests a cut from the long shot of the character running to a detail of his running feet, which begin to jump up out of frame so we can then cut to a close

shot of the character landing in his seat. Would this work? Could it be made to look convincing? I had no doubt that the shots would all cut together to make a reasonably convincing continuity, but in dramatic terms what would the shot of the feet add? It would neither impart new information nor give greater insight – in short there would be no dramatic justification for cutting to the character's feet. In the event, what we arrived at was a perfect example of an editing solution to an animation problem: we decided to cut directly from the long shot of the character running to the close shot of him landing in his vehicle. It worked beautifully, propelling the action forward and maintaining the energy and pace of the sequence.

'Having said all this, as far as possible the editing of an animated film should be approached in the same way as that of a live-action film. The grammar of visual storytelling applies. We are still dealing with actions, reactions, motivations and emotions, and the editor's job is to meld these elements into a dramatically satisfying whole through the selection, juxtaposition and timing of the material provided. Bold and, sometimes, painful decisions have to be made and some of these can involve painstakingly produced footage being cut from the film. People may not see it this way at the time (and there's a good chance you may be overruled), but the best service anyone can give the animators and everyone else working on the film is to make it the best film possible.'

The Animator as Director

The animation director operates in much the same way as the live-action director in that the work is normally the vision of that person, and the personnel attached to a project needs to be directed to facilitate the director's requirements. In animation, though, the director is very often 'hands on', too, actually animating.

Martin Pullen is a highly experienced animator and director of children's animation, from *Paddington Bear* to his own creation *Tom and Vicky*. In having clear knowledge of the demands of the animator and how this relates to the needs of the director, here he offers some insights to both roles, and talks about the creative agenda for *Tom and Vicky*.

Comparing CGI and Stop-Motion

—

Pullen: 'People who do stop-motion hate sitting at a desk or at a computer all day long. The process of CG is similar with key positions and in-betweens and so forth, but it is so boring! I need a real puppet under hot lights all day; actually touching, actually moving it and creating a physical end result. I animated and directed at Filmfair, sometimes working with four animators on a programme. I did storyboards and framed-up shots, and talked animators through the blocking. You have to delegate to a crew and work as a team because of the volume of work needed. In live action you direct

actors, but in animation you have to direct a person to move a puppet a certain way in accordance with the storyboard, and in relation to how you anticipate cutting a story together. If a shot is 200 frames long and has some specific dialogue, you need to trust the animator to execute that; other more complex moves might need particular direction.'

A Team Spirit

—

'Being able to work as part of a team is vital. Everyone must enjoy the job and bring their creativity to it. In stop-frame, drawing is less important, but being "an actor" much more significant. You are performing through the puppet and it is crucial that you study other people to recall the gestures and looks; to know how someone walks; and to "see" the timing in someone's movement. People say I stare at them, but I love to observe the details of eyes, nose and mouth in an expression, and then bring that personality to the puppet.'

Tom and Vicky

—

'I was trying to develop an idea and one day I saw a child's drawing and thought you could do something in the style of a three-dimensional child's drawing, making props out of calico and using big stitches, crayons etc. I thought I could do that myself. I thought that I would set it in a garden with two young children – Tom and Vicky – cared for by their grandad. I did designs for the main characters – a pet dog and a pet cat; then I thought, what do you get in a garden? So I came up with a pond and from that, two frogs emerged. I really wanted to focus on "style", so the look would be significantly different, and I knew I could make a pilot. As I was watching TV or travelling on a bus I would be making props and eventually, within a year, I got the puppets made and developed a pilot, which I took to Central TV. Everyone really liked it, but it was eventually financed by Granada and ITV commissioned it.

'Central to it were the frogs, Fred and Bert. I loved the children's animation *The Herbs*, where all the characters had a signature song, so I thought we would put a song in every episode. The stories were quite fantastical, but they would often start with a sort of logical starting place, for example, Tom and Vicky looking for a pot of gold at the end of the rainbow, or hunting for dinosaur bones, or encountering the squid who lived in the pond – fish are such a pain to animate, I thought it would be more fun! All right, it is my Harryhausen moment as well, but he's a squid who lives in an old tugboat and knows everything, and the frogs are behaving like Laurel and Hardy, so the combination of "know-it-all" and foolishness really works. There were 26 shows and they were very popular. I think children liked the tactility and invention of it.'

PART

Applications and Outcomes

Learning how to animate and make animated films is best done through a combination of reading the available literature, taking the advice and support of others with more experience and knowledge, and doing as much 'hands on' practice as possible.

However, it is important to reiterate that all creative practice needs a great deal of thought and preparation, as well as technique. There is no practice without theory and no theory without practice. Bringing together historical knowledge, conceptual and technical insight, and the desire to create something distinctive is crucial, but not necessarily enough. Being able to articulate the 'art' of creative practice, as well as demonstrating it through the work, is a vital component in proving its worth and effect.

This section offers an historical and critical context for the four core disciplines of animation – drawn/cel; 3D puppet/clay stop-motion; computer generated; and 'alternative' or 'experimental' animation – and draws upon the work of students and professionals across the animation disciplines, with discussions about the working process. Consequently, it offers a range of insights and 'best practice', which will be highly valuable to anyone embarking on making an animated film.

8.2

Still from *Gertie the Dinosaur* – Winsor McCay

Gertie, who featured in Winsor McCay's vaudeville routine, was arguably the first example of the kind of 'personality' animation much admired and developed by Disney. The dinosaur clearly had an identity and point of view of its own, and was very appealing and amusing to audiences.

A Brief History

—

As early as 1913, John R. Bray and Raoul Barré were developing systematic, 'industrial' processes for the production of animated cartoons using variations of what was to become the 'cel' animation process, where individual drawings, later cels, were created with various stages of a character's forward movement, and these were aligned with backgrounds that remained the same, using a peg-bar system: by replacing each stage of the movement and photographing it frame by frame, the illusion of continuous movement occurred. More importantly, a production system was emerging that echoed the economies and hierarchical organisation of Taylorist production processes that characterised the industrial progress of modern America, most notably, in the production of Model T Fords at the Henry Ford car plants. Though the Fleischer Brothers, Paul Terry and Pat Sullivan with Otto Messmer, all emerged as viable producers of cartoons, it was Walt Disney who effectively took the Ford model and created an animation 'industry'.

With *Steamboat Willie* (1928), Disney, in the face of increased competition from the technically adept Fleischer Studio, created the first fully synchronised sound cartoon, simultaneously introducing animation's first cartoon superstar, Mickey Mouse. Within ten years, Disney had made *Snow White and the Seven Dwarfs* (1937), the first full-length, sound-synchronised, Technicolor animated film, along the way making the seminal *Silly Symphonies*, including *Flowers and Trees* (1932), the first cartoon made in three-strip Technicolor; *Three Little Pigs* (1933); *The Band Concert* (1935); *The Country Cousin* (1936); and *The Old Mill* (1937), all of which made aesthetic, technical and narrative strides in the field. Disney effectively defined animation and created a legacy that all other producers learn from, respond to and seek to imitate or challenge. As Disney made *Pinocchio* (1940) and *Fantasia* (1941), the Warner

Bros. studio continued its emergence, and following the Disney strike of 1941 (which arguably ended 'the Golden Era' of animation), provided a context in which Chuck Jones, Frank Tashlin, Tex Avery, Bob Clampett and Friz Freleng became the new heirs to the animated short. Altogether more urban and adult, the Warner Bros. cartoons were highly inventive, redefining the situational 'gags' in Disney films through a higher degree of surreal, self-reflexive and taboo-breaking humour. While the Fleischers had Betty Boop, and a strong embrace of Black culture and underground social mores, and Hanna-Barbera had the enduring Tom and Jerry, Warner Bros. had the zany Daffy Duck, the laconic 'wise ass' Bugs Bunny and gullible dupes Porky Pig and Elmer Fudd, who became popular and morale-raising figures during the war-torn 1940s and its aftermath.

Jones and Avery, in particular, altered the aesthetics of the cartoon, changing its pace and subject matter, relying less on the 'full animation' of Disney, and more on different design strategies and self-conscious thematic concerns, for example, sex and sexuality; injustice; status and social position. In many senses, the innovation in cartoons as varied as *The Dover Boys* (1942), *Red Hot Riding Hood* (1943) and *Coal Black and de Sebben Dwarfs* (1943) anticipates the more formal experimentation of the UPA (United Productions of America) studio, a breakaway group of Disney animators, including Steve Bosustow, Dave Hilberman and Zachary Schwartz, wishing to work more in the style of modernist art (actually pioneered at the Halas & Batchelor and Larkins Studios in England), less in the comic vein, and on more auteurist terms and conditions. Works like *Gerald McBoing Boing* (1951) and *The Tell-Tale Heart* (1953) used minimalist backgrounds and limited animation, and were clearly embracing a European modernist sensibility that itself was developing in the 'reduced animation' of the Zagreb Studios, and its leading artist Dusan Vukotic.

As the Disney studio arguably entered a period of decline, Chuck Jones created three masterpieces – *Duck Amuck* (1953), *One Froggy Evening* (1956) and *What's Opera, Doc?* (1957) – all exhibiting Jones's ability to deconstruct the cartoon, work with literate and complex themes, and create cartoon 'art' in its own right.

8.3

***Fritz the Cat* – Ralph Bakshi**

Bakshi's counter-culture cartoon for adults was taboo breaking and subversive in its representation of a sexualised, drug-taking, politically aware America in the shape of cartoon animals, previously the epitome of innocence and child-friendly humour.

8.4

Akira –Katsuhiro Ôtomo

Ôtomo's breakthrough animé is distinguished by its dystopian feel and its spectacular animation sequences, which revolutionised animated feature animation and brought a new audience to the form.

In retrospect, it is clear that these were the last great works of the theatrical era, as the major studios closed their short cartoon units and the television era began. It is pertinent to note, too, that Halas & Batchelor's adaptation of George Orwell's *Animal Farm* (1954) had also progressed the cartoon feature, addressing serious subject matter and representing animals in a more realistic and less 'Disneyfied' way. Many critics see the Saturday morning cartoon era as the true demise of the American cartoonal tradition, but

arguably, especially in the pioneering efforts of the Hanna-Barbera studio, it was the very versatility of animation as an expressive vocabulary that enabled its continuity at a time when its cost might have prevented its survival altogether.

At the same time, the Japanese animation industry expanded its production specifically for the television market, and series like *Astro Boy* debuted on US television. Echoing the popularity of manga in

Japanese culture, animé of all kinds have emerged in the post-war period, and by the early 1980s Japanese studios were producing some 400 series for the global TV market; by the early 1990s over 100 features were produced a year. Katsuhiro Ôtomo's *Akira* (Manga Entertainment, 1988) was the 'breakthrough' animé, which introduced Western audiences to the complex, multi-narrative, apocalyptic agendas of much Japanese animation, and the works of Hayao Miyazaki, Mamoru Oshii and Masamune Shirow that followed competed with Disney, Dreamworks and PIXAR in the global feature marketplace. Filmation and Hanna-Barbera continued to produce cartoons for American television, and Disney consolidated its place in the new medium with Disneyland and later variations like Walt Disney's Wonderful World of Color. Individual works continued to emerge from the National Film Board of Canada (NFBC), established in the early 1940s by John Grierson and led by the innovative Norman McLaren, but in the American context, radicalisation appeared in the frame of Ralph Bakshi, who explored adult themes and the spirit of the late 1960s counterculture in his sexually explicit and racially charged films *Fritz the Cat* (1972), *Heavy Traffic* (1973) and *Coonskin* (1975). In effect, this was the first time that animation in America was used by adults to engage adults with contemporary adult issues and cultural politics.

Jimmy Murakami's adaptation of Raymond Briggs's *When the Wind Blows* (1986), like *Animal Farm* (1954) and *Yellow Submarine* (1968), represented attempts in Britain to innovate in the traditional 2D cartoon, but it was Hayao Miyazaki in *Laputa, the Flying Island* (1986), *My Neighbour Totoro* (1988) and *Porco Rosso* (1992) who sustained and enhanced the quality of the animated feature, and the partnership of Ron Clements and John Musker with *The Little Mermaid* (1989),

Aladdin (1992) and *Hercules* (1997), who revived Disney's fortunes. While the cartoon short enjoyed continuing innovation in the work of Paul Driessen, Cordell Barker and Richard Condie at the NFBC, it was clear that the impact of digital technologies would revise the animated feature, and indeed, production for television. The TV cartoon has enjoyed a renaissance in the works of Ben Bocquelet (*The Amazing World of Gumball*), Pendleton Ward (*Adventure Time*) and several reboots of classic series like Aardman Animation's *The New Adventures of Morph* (2014) and Boulder Media's *Danger Mouse* (2015) series. Matt Groening's *The Simpsons* has become a national institution, but feature animation essentially changed with the success of PIXAR's *Toy Story* (1995), the first fully computer-generated animated feature, and the subsequent success of its sequels (*Toy Story 2*, 1999, *Toy Story 3*, 2010) and of films like *Frozen* (2013) and *Inside Out* (2015).

Walk Cycles

—

One of the core practices in drawn animation is the walk cycle – essentially the 'benchmark' model of movement that is pertinent to other depictions of physical activity in animation.

Creating walk cycles and activity in motion is fundamental to the craft of animation. Motion studies created by Eadweard Muybridge are still a valuable source in achieving such movement, which in the early years of animation was drawn and captured by painting on cels.

TUTORIAL

Walk Cycles

—

In a book of this length it is not possible to include tutorials on a range of technical approaches, but over the next few pages a consideration of the 'walk cycle' will be undertaken by Arril Johnson, as it is one of the traditional and key aspects of animation, which should be mastered by all aspiring animators.

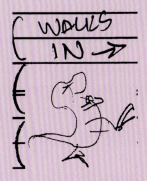

Diagram 1

This detail from a dope sheet shows a thumbnail sketch of Feldspar the dinosaur not just walking, but walking with attitude. Think about the length of the step the character takes. Is it a long, bold step? Is it a short, tired shuffle? Think about the speed of the step. Is it slow and fearful? Slow and lazy? Quick and nervous? Quick and aggressive? Or is it just average and relaxed? When walking, as in Diagram 2, does the character lead with its head, its chest, its pelvis or its feet? Does it walk in a flat-footed way or does it have an adolescent bounce? What is its purpose and mood?

Diagram 2

Generally, when a series of drawings is produced showing the right foot swinging forward while the left foot slides back and then the left swinging forward while the right slides back, the foot doing the sliding while it bears the weight of the character will slide in regularly spaced stages. This is because this collection of drawings, called a 'walk cycle', is usually designed for use over a panning background that pans in a consistent and fluid way. This is done in order to create the illusion of a camera following the character as the character walks along in front of the background.

The same set of drawings and background can be used in another way; the character can walk forward into, through, and out of the scene while the background remains static.

The point is, once the foot supporting the character's weight is placed on 'ground', its position relative to the background is fixed until it can be lifted up for the forward swing.

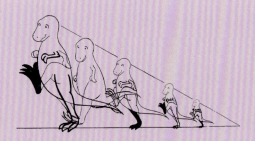

Diagram 9

This is a simplified plan for a character running forward in three-quarter view. Initially, a master or key drawing was prepared, which showed the character with a double set of limbs so that the alternate positions of the left and right feet, for example, could be seen in one graphic. This was constructed within a wedge that matched the required perspective of the character's path. In this case the drawing was copied over three generations and each time reduced to about 65 per cent of its previous size. Of course, a reduction in size has no effect on the angle of the wedge and so it was then possible to easily position the three copies where they needed to be within the wedge of the original drawing. Now that a rigid framework existed to control the perspective and proportions of the character's key positions, the required in-between drawings could be improvised in order to give a more organic and varied feeling to the final animation.

Diagram 10

Of course, there are other ways to get to where you're going.

Muybridging

—

Here is a movement sequence based on Muybridge's horse gallop – essentially a core sequence of eight repeating movements, showing the shifting dynamics of bodily weight, compression and extension through the stride pattern.

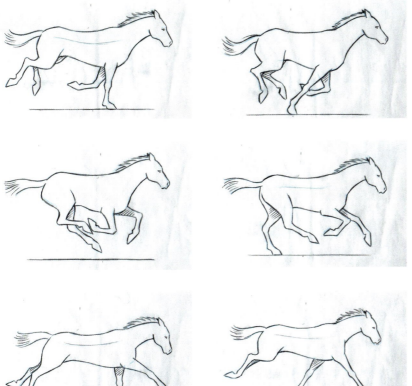

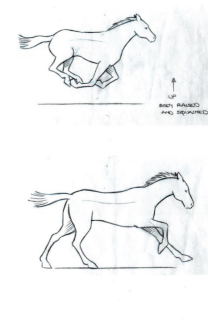

8.5

Cels for a gallop sequence from the Animation Workshop, The Animation Academy, Loughborough University, UK.

Drawing and Aesthetic Tradition

—

There are different traditions of 'drawing' in animation that respond to the indigenous traditions of the arts in any one nation. Here is an example of the ways traditional drawn animation works in a Japanese context.

Koji Yamamura's work is effectively 'anti-animé' – a response to what is an increasingly mainstream, homogenised, industrial product, boasting some outstanding figures like Tezuka, Miyazaki, Oshii, Ôtomo and Shirow, but nevertheless characterised by many forgettable genre movies. Yamamura returns to an indigenous, traditional Rakugo (comic strip) story, Atama-yama, for his multi-award winning short film, *Mt. Head*, which tells of a mean-spirited man who swallows a cherry pip and grows a cherry tree out of his head.

Metamorphosis

—

Yamamura's return to a traditional narrative is accompanied by a return to traditional hand-drawn animation. This privileges his particular skill in using metamorphosis, as one thing transforms into another, enabling a sometimes literal space to become an emotional space or even the realm of fantasy or dream, without any of the elements being discernably different. Is the cherry tree a metaphor for the man's psychological state? Is it a charming and surreal storytelling device? Is it a vehicle to play out oppositional tensions between nature and culture, reality and fantasy, bureaucracy and art, life and death?

Yamamura's experience

—

Clearly, the film works on a number of levels. The film was completed over two years and is composed of over 10,000 drawings.

Yamamura: 'First I worked for a while at the company of animation background art, then I quit and started to make my own animation films. I have learned all animation by myself. When I was 13 I read a column on how to make an animation film using Super 8. That was a start, and I have kept making my own animation for fun. While I studied Fine Art at Tokyo Zokei University, I saw the retrospective of Ishu Patel at the first Animation festival in Hiroshima in 1985. That made me decide to create animation films as my life work. I had worked for ten years to make short animations for children, but from the start I had always wished to make shorts that adults can enjoy. The theme throughout *Mt. Head* was a recognition of a mystery of life and an absurdity that you can never handle rationally.'

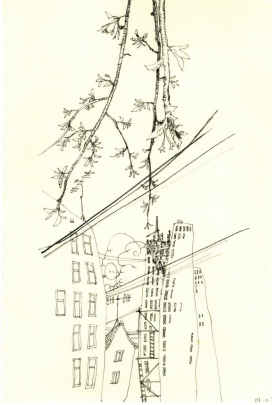

**8.8
Sketches and stills
from *Mt. Head* –
Koji Yamamura**

3D Stop-motion Animation

3D stop-motion animation has two distinct histories. The first is the largely European tradition of short stop-motion films made by individual artists, and stop-motion series principally made for children's television. The second, and predominantly Hollywood tradition, is the 'invisible' history of stop-motion animation as a branch of special effects for feature-length films. This is complicated further by the fact that 3D stop-motion animation has got two principal approaches using either puppets or clay models, but also includes films made with objects and artefacts.

A Brief History

—

Though J. Stuart Blackton and Albert E. Smith, Britons working in the USA, have been credited with making the first puppet film – called *The Humpty Dumpty Circus* (1908) – there remains the possibility that British film-maker Arthur Melbourne-Cooper may have made the first 3D advertisement as early as 1899, called *Matches: An Appeal*, animating matches, an approach shared in Émile Cohl's 1908 film, *The Animated Matches*. Cooper's 'toys come to life' stories became a staple of early British animated film and included *Dreams of Toyland* (1908) and *The Toymaker's Dream* (1913). Similar preoccupations informed Giovanni Pastrone's *The War and the Dreams of Momi* (1913) and later, Alexander Ptushko in *The New Gulliver* (1935), but it was another Russian, Ladislaw Starewicz, who first developed an extraordinary technique, following his interest in entomology, animating three-dimensional insect characters. *The Cameraman's Revenge* (1911) is a melodramatic love triangle, and highly self-conscious in its reflexive tale of cinema about cinema. His later films, *Town Rat, Country Rat* (1926) and *Tale of the Fox* (1930/released 1938), are masterpieces of the stop-motion form, and remained singularly unsung until recent years.

Not Disney

Animation made outside the American cartoonal tradition, and the long shadow of Disney, has often been marginalised in animation histories. This does more than neglect important, aesthetically different work; it dismisses significant indigenous works that reflect national cultures and alternative perspectives on human experience. It is also true to say that the American tradition, particularly in its formative years, is largely a comic tradition. Other countries have aspired to different kinds of storytelling and have different thematic and artistic preoccupations. The recovery of this work is essential to a full understanding of the place of animation not merely in international film culture and history, but as an articulation of the distinctiveness and diversity of the art form in general.

In the USA, though, it was pioneer Willis O'Brien who inspired generations of what would be called 'effects artists'. Amused by his brother's playful changing some of the postures of clay figures created for the exhibits in the San Francisco World Fair of 1915, O'Brien experimented with his first stop-motion film of a boxing match, soon to be followed by a prehistoric 'comedy', *The Dinosaur and the Missing Link* (1915). In 1925 he made *The Lost World*, based on a Sir Arthur Conan Doyle story, assisted by gifted model-maker Marcel Delgado, who constructed 18" models influenced by Charles Knight's acclaimed dinosaur paintings in the American Museum of Natural History. RKO then employed O'Brien on the ground-breaking *King Kong* (1933), which changed the status of special effects work, fully deploying O'Brien's 'rear projection' system, which combined background live action with foreground miniature animation, first seen in O'Brien's aborted project, *The Creation* (1930).

9.1

King Kong – **Merian C. Cooper & Ernest B. Schoedsack**

Willis O'Brien's ground-breaking stop-motion animation in *King Kong* proved profoundly influential on generations of film-makers from Ray Harryhausen to Phil Tippett to Barry Purves to Peter Jackson.

123

The special effects tradition

The special effects tradition is often understood in a way that effaces important work. Even though an audience is required to embrace the spectacle of an effect, it is crucial that it seems authentic enough for it to seem 'invisible' as an effect in the live-action context it is presented within. This has also had the consequence of marginalising a great deal of animation work, and its major artists. While Ray Harryhausen is now properly lauded, it is nevertheless still the case that his work is seen as 'old fashioned' and of another time. For stop-motion animators, it is crucial that his work is viewed as 'state of the art'; his technique in regard to the movement of full bodies, often with multiple limbs, and complex actions, is still unsurpassed.

Harryhausen's legacy is great, but George Pal, his one-time employer, also exemplified fine work. His 'replacement' technique was of a slightly different order. Where Harryhausen manipulated his models by small increments and recorded them frame by frame, Pal created replacement pieces of his models – faces, arms, legs etc. – which progressed the cycle of movement he was creating, and which he changed and inserted, once more recording the incremental progression frame by frame. Though a more cumbersome technique, it survives into the modern era, particularly in clay animation, and has been used in films by Aardman Animation. After making early films in Germany, Pal moved to Holland, fleeing the rise of Nazism, and established the biggest puppet studio in Europe, principally making striking advertisements for sponsors like Philips and Unilever. His Puppetoons, made in Hollywood, included *Jasper and the Beanstalk* (1945), *Henry and the Inky Poo* (1946) and *Tubby the Tuba* (1947), and were highly successful, securing Pal a reputation that enabled him to produce and direct feature-length sci-fi and fantasy films like *The War of the Worlds* (1953), *Tom Thumb* (1958), *The Time Machine* (1960) and *The Wonderful World of the Brothers Grimm* (1963).

Pal's legacy in Europe has been sustained, consolidated and advanced by two major figures of Czechoslovakian origin. Influenced by the indigenous marionette and theatrical traditions, Jiří Trnka and Jan Svankmajer have produced a range of extraordinary films pushing the boundaries not merely of the stop-motion technique, but of other approaches, too. Trnka's were politicised if romantic-vision inspired masterpieces like *Old Czech Legends* (1953), *A Midsummer Night's Dream* (1955) and *The Hand* (1965), while Svankmajer's more subversive and challenging view, genuinely taboo-breaking in its daring, meant he created films like *Dimensions of Dialogue* (1982), *Alice* (1987) and *Little Otik* (2001). This altogether darker work was to inspire the Quay Brothers working in England; Kihachiro Kawamoto working in Japan; and Tim Burton and Henry Selick working in the USA.

Concept-driven animation

Jan Svankmajer's work is an important example of the ways in which the principles of modernist thought and political insight may be accommodated in experimental film. Svankmajer's 'agit-prop' – his strident critique of authoritarian regimes and political repression – and 'agit-scare' – his use of surreal images drawn from the unconscious to prompt moments of fear and revelation in his audience – are conceptual applications to the medium and should be understood as a methodology in the creation of distinctive imagery and alternative narratives. By adopting a 'conceptual' premise to an animation, a highly original outcome can sometimes be achieved.

The contemporary era has seen the emergence of the Will Vinton studios in America and Aardman Animation in the UK as masters of clay animation. The two styles vary, but both studios value the 'clay' aesthetic as something visually distinctive and engaging. Nick Park, Aardman's most famous son, has created Wallace, the eccentric inventor, and his altogether smarter dog, Gromit, a now globally famous partnership, that has featured in Park's shorts, *A Grand Day Out* (1989), *The Wrong Trousers* (1993) and *A Close Shave* (1995). Park's work, though speaking to a wider tradition of English wit and whimsy, nevertheless has clear affiliations with the stop-motion animation made for children's television in the UK by Gordon Murray and Bura and Hardwick – *Camberwick Green* (1966) and *Trumpton* (1967); Oliver Postgate and Peter Firman – *The Clangers* (1969) and *Bagpuss* (1974); and Ivor Wood at Filmfair – *The Wombles* (1973) and *Postman Pat* (1981). The high quality of three-dimensional animation for children in the UK has been sustained by Cosgrove Hall, S4C and BBC Animation, and

has only been echoed in the American context by the early 1960s work of Jules Bass – *Rudolph the Red-Nosed Reindeer* (1964) and *Mad Monster Party* (1968) – and Art Clokey's simple clay figure, *Gumby* (1955 onwards). Inevitably, Will Vinton's *Martin the Cobbler* (1976), *The Adventures of Mark Twain* (1985) and the 1990s' advertisements for the Californian Raisin Advisory Board, featuring raisins singing popular songs, have in their various ways created a benchmark in clay animation in the USA, which has always had to compete with the Disney tradition, but also in recent years with the now dominant CGI aesthetic.

The fundamental belief in the sheer 'difference' and visual appeal of stop-motion animation has also prompted the emergence of important individual artists, from Serge Danot – *The Magic Roundabout* (1965) – to Joan Gratz – *Mona Lisa Descending a Staircase* (1992) – to Barry Purves – *Gilbert & Sullivan* (1999), each bringing a specific vision to the materials, sense of theatrical space and fluid timing of their narratives.

The craft aesthetic

Stop-motion and clay animators have always championed the 'materiality' and 'textural' aspects of their work as the distinctive appeal of 3D stop-motion, but one of the most significant aspects remains the necessarily 'artisanal' approach to the work, which is not reliant on 'off the shelf' software, but on the ability to make and build things, as well as to respond to the miniature demands of theatrical practice and live-action film-making techniques on a small scale.

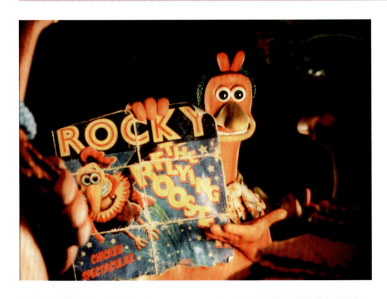

9.4

Stills from _Chicken Run_ – Peter Lord & Nick Park

Chicken Run (Aardman Animations, 2000), Aardman's parody of _The Great Escape_ and other Second World War movies, combines English eccentricity and whimsy with Hollywood-style spectacle and adventure, sustaining the tradition of 3D stop-motion into the contemporary era.

Sound and Stop-motion Animation

—

Master animator Barry Purves sees a strong relationship between sound and the sense of performance in stop-motion animation, preferring nuanced vocal performances, specific and suggestive sound effects, and, above all, an inspiring musical score to create a distinctive soundtrack for animation.

Purves: 'Like most elements that make up animated films, sound is usually a celebration of artifice. In my own films I am personally reluctant to use straightforward dialogue, as this inevitably leads to a static, talking-heads approach to shooting (that's a bit of a naive generalisation, but not untrue). I favour a more movement-based form of storytelling, seeing the whole body of the character as much as possible – using the body language to tell the drama and emotion. I guess I find a body more interesting than a generally over-animated mouth flapping away.'

Using artificial constructs

—

'I prefer to use words, not as dialogue, but in enjoyably artificial constructs like singing (in my *Rigoletto* and *Gilbert & Sullivan* films), or stylised nods towards Kabuki (*Screen Play*) or Greek drama (*Achilles*). It has to be said that a lot of my favourite short animated films, like *The Monk and the Fish*, and *Three Misses*, are wordless.'

The cliché of voices for animation

—

'When I have worked with voice artists I definitely try to avoid the usual characterisation of animated characters – wildly over the top and silly cartoony voices. This may seem to contradict my words about celebrating the artifice, but nothing would make me switch off quicker than squeaky vocal gymnastics. These untruthful performances, on way too many shows to mention, are not the same as honest and detailed character work, such as *The Simpsons*, however flamboyant they may be. The voices in *Babe* strike me as some of the most beautiful voice acting I have heard for ages. They manage to suggest the animal as well as the human qualities, without ever having to resort to cheap tricks.'

Methods of voice recording

—

'With working with voices, I prefer to have the whole cast in one room and allow them to bounce off each other, and happily let them tread on each others' sentences and fluff the odd line; it's these unexpected details that seem to make a character live. Obviously, it is sometimes impractical to have the cast all together, but I'd always encourage some spontaneity from the actor. I'd also be very specific about the physicality of the situation … I hate those moments when the clearly static voice performance in a studio bears no relation to the physical efforts of the character in the film.'

Lip-synching

—

'Lip-synch is something that seems to get students and young animators bogged down. I think I would probably concentrate on the eye acting than over-synched mouth shapes. It is the eyes we watch in a conversation and too often than not, we do not have the necessary anatomy on an animated character (such as teeth, or a tongue) to do accurate lip-synch. We don't have enough frames in a second either. The secret probably is to suggest the mouth shapes, suggesting the syllables rather than meticulously closing and shutting the mouth with every letter. The rhythm and vocal effort are probably more important than accuracy.'

The value of impressionistic sound

—

'Likewise with sound effects. It's all too easy to add an effect for every rustle of clothing or every footstep. This leads to a very cluttered soundtrack, especially as music is nearly always an essential element. And, again, I'd suggest that often the effects are too literal. Since we are playing with things of the imagination, we have the freedom to surprise, to emphasise, and to challenge the expected. It is inevitable that sound effects usually get left to the end of production, and added when filming is finished, but I'd encourage the use of sound as a storytelling element in its own right, and not just as atmosphere. I'm afraid I find that for most colleges, working with sound is usually an afterthought. As a practical point, sound can often be used to suggest things that the budget won't allow to be seen, and is often the more effective and surprising for that.'

Music

—

'And as for music, several chapters should be devoted to this essential element of storytelling. It's often music that starts me thinking about a film, and I love the discipline of using a precise, fixed piece of music. Having the musical score at the start of a film certainly works for me, and probably stops the composer's frustration of having to make his or her music fit with mathematics. Music seems to focus me and allows me to make every moment count, as well as giving the films a natural rhythm and flow. I've seldom used music just as background, and have always been lucky to have specially composed or recorded music. To me, it is just as important a part of the storytelling as the visuals, and this has occasionally, only occasionally, led to conflict in the mixing where most engineers are used to TV dramas and insist in putting the music timidly "behind" the picture. To me, it is right there up front. Animation, in my eyes, is a great marriage and celebration of movement, music and design, all equally telling the story and illuminating the characters. I think that is why I respond to ballet and dance so instinctively and constantly refer to animation as a relation of dance.'

AUTHOR TIP

Movement as meaning

Express as much narrative information as possible through looks, gesture and physical movement that has a particular purpose or objective.

9.5

Stills from *Rigoletto* – Barry Purves

Purves uses the tight construction and specificity of the musical score to help him structure the dynamics of the dramatic performance in his animation. He concentrates on the physical gestures of characters as the determining emotional vocabulary of his work, each figure literally embodying the suggested feelings in the musical narrative.

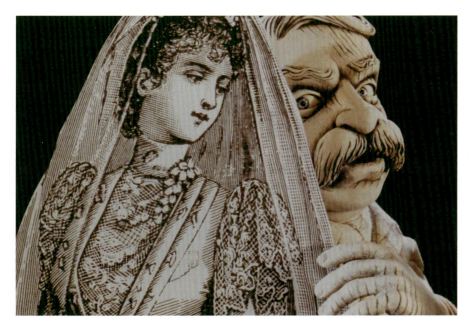

9.6

Still from *Gilbert and Sullivan: The Very Models* – Barry Purves

The wit and whimsy of a range of Gilbert and Sullivan operettas is combined in a musical narrative, which tells the story of Gilbert and Sullivan themselves. Purves illustrates this combinative score with the rich textures of design drawn from the staging of the D'Oyly Carte performances.

Enunciation

'Enunciation' in animation sounds a more complex concept than it actually is. Simply, when animation comes on the cinema, television or computer screen, the audience 'knows it' to be animation. The form has got such a distinctive 'look', 'feel' and 'style' that it literally 'announces' itself, and in doing so shows a scale of artifice or illusion that implies the presence of a creator – the animator or auteur.

Strategic choice of media

—

Celebrity Deathmatch gained high viewing ratings and led to Fogel being named in *Entertainment Weekly's* top 100 most creative people in the industry. It is certainly clear that Fogel's commitment to stop-motion animation was not merely an aesthetic decision but a political one too, as he saw the advent of computer-generated animation and the huge investment in it by all the major studios as potentially endangering the survival of the process. Having committed to stop-motion, it was clear, however, that for the fast turnaround required for a television series, it would be necessary to eliminate the use of clay because the wear and tear was extensive, and the consequent degeneration of the characters meant the time-consuming necessity of re-sculpting. Having addressed this issue, the team making the show, some 20 full-time animators, worked on 15 sound stages, producing 10 seconds of animation per day, and a half-hour show in five weeks, sometimes using elaborate wire systems for 'flying' characters that echo the full-scale use of similar processes to create spectacular imagery, drawn from Hong Kong cinema, in live-action works like *The Matrix* and *Crouching Tiger, Hidden Dragon*.

The process

—

The animation is created against chromatic backgrounds, and various 'plates' of crowd characters from an archive of audience responses are digitally mixed with the key action in the computer. While computers are an integral part of the process, it is important to stress that Fogel most values the importance of pre-production and the work of the scriptwriting teams, and the singular and distinctive 'authorship' in manipulating one frame at a time.

Influences

—

Fogel: 'Growing up, I had a love affair with animation in general, but I soon realised that there was work that I liked which was not the "kiddie-toon" stuff you would find on a Saturday morning. We had something in the States called Science Fiction Theatre on Saturday afternoons, and on those sort of programmes you would find the work of Ray Harryhausen – Sinbad movies and such – and there was one particular movie, *The Mysterious Island*, where you had a gigantic

crab crawling up out of the sand and attacking the tiny people. I was always frustrated and amazed at the same time, because without the aid of a VCR you could not pause the animation and study it, and you had no means to find out the "tricks" – how was it done – so I was mystified and delighted, and knew that I wanted to find out about the process of animation, and become an animator.'

Various comedic approaches

—

'I got behind a camera and experimented. I have an art background in the sense that I always sketched, doodled and sculpted – it wasn't traditional, in the sense that I wasn't trained. Everything that I have learned was achieved through experience. I was always a fan of professional wrestling because those characters seemed to me to be so much like cartoon characters, so much larger than life, and then there was another show out of the UK called *Spitting Image*, and during the 1980s they were running these specials in the States, and I remember seeing the Ronald Reagan and Michael Jackson caricatures, and finding them so well observed and funny. Just the image of these already exaggerated people as puppets blew me away, so I thought if I combined these two elements – the wrestling and the celebrity satire – it would make a great stop-motion series. Animation has always embraced different kinds of approach to comedy, and satire, while attractive to the animator, can also create problems if mishandled.

'On the one hand, if you do it incorrectly, you can come across as mean-spirited or angry, and we did not want that to happen; all we wanted to do was to have fun, and laugh at these characters at their expense, and that was a much easier sell in animation. Also these celebrities are proud to be seen that way; being represented in animation is like a vain tribute to their work. Before I got to MTV I had been developing the idea for about a year and just as I was about to prepare to finance the first short films, I was fortunate that MTV decided that they would go ahead, and we made the first fight – Charles Manson versus Marilyn Manson. We knew that we would only have two weeks to make this five-minute animation and it was only myself and one other animator doing the work, and we knew that clay was not going to work. I had worked with clay a lot in the past and I knew that within the timeframe available that it would slow us down tremendously. Again, with this first fight, we knew it was essentially a pilot, a test, so we had a model shop create foam latex versions of the clay puppets and it proved much more efficient to work with these models. We still used clay heads to sculpt the good expressions and get the exaggerated reactions that we wanted, and when we wanted to do extreme reactions, we made a series of replaceable heads and actually sculpted the expression into a series of six heads, sometimes combining these heads with a digital morph. Later on, we went on to use resin heads to preserve the look of clay and reduce the weight of the head so it would not keep tipping over, but we kept the area around the eyes soft so that we could still sculpt there and widen the expressions. We also manipulate the eyebrows and change the mouth; these are the only things that are moveable on the heads.'

9.8

Stills from Philips Broadcast of 1938 – George Pal

One of Fogel's seminal influences, George Pal, created animated advertisements, which, like *Celebrity Deathmatch*, playfully parodied elements of Hollywood culture, from movie stars to dance crazes and subcultures.

While embracing the techniques of George Pal and Ray Harryhausen, Fogel also readily engaged with new production software.

Fogel: 'We are using the same technology as we were when we started off – we use Adobe Premiere to capture the animation and Adobe After Effects to apply the digital effects. These are off-the-shelf software packages, but what has happened is that our digital team has got better through doing, and this has improved the look. They are constantly using different kinds of software to improve the visual impact of the work, and I am always looking for shots that we can enhance digitally, to make them more memorable, and ways to enhance the animation. We completed a Halloween special, for example. We have a character growing – it starts as a skull on the floor and slowly morphs into a full-sized human, and you see all the layers of anatomy – the flesh, the muscle, the skin – everything is growing from the skull and expanding into the limbs, the arms and the legs. We use a combination of on-set clay-sculpting for the musculature; then morphing to make the transition between several replaceable bodies; and then we had a 2D artist treat the musculature with a variety of techniques, and this is combined in one shot. It was amazing! Metamorphosis is still the central preoccupation of the art, I think.'

Celebrity Deathmatch has been extraordinarily successful with both the public and the figures it playfully satires. As Fogel says, 'We had an extraordinary response from Steven Spielberg when we pitted him against Alfred Hitchcock – of course, he had to lose to "the Master" – but he wrote to us demanding a re-match, so that was a great moment.'

NOTES

4. The Erasmus scheme works across Europe and enables higher education students to study or work abroad as part of their degree, and staff to teach or train in 33 European countries. See http://ec.europa.eu/programmes/erasmus-plus/index_en.htm.

A First Experience

—

Students aspiring to be animators arrive at the subject from many different routes. Techniques are many and varied but studying at university gives student animators the opportunity to experiment with different techniques and practices.

The Fisherman and the Cat was an MA project undertaken by Polish student Katarzyna (Kate) Sejud at the University of Wolverhampton, UK. Katarzyna was interested in drawing and painting from a young age, and so when she left school applied for a graphic design internship. She then studied on a photography and multimedia degree course in Poland and as part of the course did some classes in animation. She said, 'I realised that I could draw but I couldn't animate really, so I began to do some simple model and puppet animation, and I thought – yeah, I can do it!'

In her second year she concentrated more on her animation, so when she took part in the Erasmus scheme[4] to study abroad, she decided to study animation. 'I like storytelling so it was a perfect match. Animation is one of the greatest arts because it combines everything, really.' On her return to Poland she wanted to continue her animation studies, so she returned to the UK to study for an MA in animation.

The Fisherman and the Cat film was developed for her MA study. 'It started with a character development module that I had taken whilst in the UK on the Erasmus scheme. We had a task to come up with two characters, and I found a photo of a sailor with a cat. I thought that the relation between the man, the sea, and the cat had something good and I would like to explore it more.' Katarzyna attempted lots of different scenarios with the characters, but eventually realised that since it was a short film she should keep it simple and clear. 'My story developed so many times, and changed *so* many times, but I hope now that it is simple and moving.'

9.9

Still from *The Fisherman and the Cat*, made by Katarzyna Sejud as part of her MA study. This was an oil-on-glass film and Kate's first experience of working using this technique.

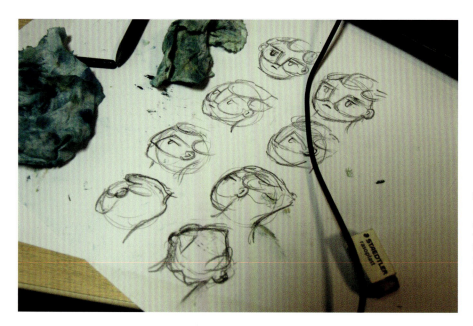

9.10

Head turn reference images for the character of the fisherman. Because the film was made under the camera it was vital to have movement images to refer to, as making the next destroyed each previous image.

The storyboarding process

—

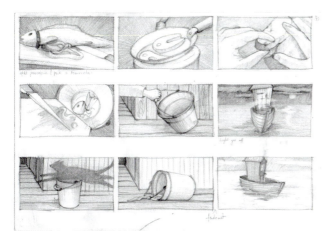

9.11

Kate used storyboarding as a helpful tool to weed out problems:
'I storyboarded if I thought the idea had potential. It helped to
see how it worked visually. I'm quite an analytical person so if I
finished the storyboard and there was something missing, I thought
about how to fix those problems and did a new version.' She said
that showing her storyboard to tutors and other students was an
important part of getting feedback on what was working: 'I needed to
see what they got from it and make sure that I was communicating
what I wanted to say. It all took time. A lot of time.'

Oil on glass technique

—

9.12

Kate chose oil paint on glass to tell her story. 'Most of the animators
that I liked [in Poland] did stop motion. When I came to the UK I
was shown more 2D work and I thought it was something I should
explore. I saw the work of Alexander Petrov and Caroline Leaf and
I thought their work was amazing. I wanted to try it and I felt really
good painting, with the textures … I used my fingers to do the
painting and I just fell in love with that technique.' It was a learning
experience as she went along. 'At first I felt very insecure making the
film, because I had no experience of working this way. Then I thought;
everyone has to have their first time, so I need to try it, because
if I don't I will regret it.' Kate felt that if she wanted to try a new
technique, using her time at university was the ideal time to do it.

Concept

—

'If you are making a children's series you've got to have a simple concept that people can grasp straight away. Basically, if you said, "What is the *Koalas* about?", I would say, it is about two koalas who fly around in a plane and help people in the Outback, that's it. So it is about "helping". BBC Worldwide really embraced this as this was what they termed "core values". That perspective was helpful because it forced me to understand exactly what the show was about and, in terms of purpose, suddenly I realised that if you are making a show that is saying "it is good to help others", that is not a bad thing to be doing because it crosses religious and political boundaries. It is not a contentious thing to say and is important enough to sustain the work across a long series.'

Execution

—

'The big thing we try to do with *The Koala Brothers* is to strip the possibilities down: it is set in a desert. I've worked on many shows where you spend 90 per cent of the time doing set dressing and lighting, and the animators get to work for 10 per cent of the time on what is in essence the most important thing of all. So we set this in the Outback, which is sky, ground and a rock, so you are spending your time on the personalities of characters, and the story. The Outback setting focuses everything on those characters, and in the real Outback the whole thing of people being isolated and having to work together, make their own entertainment, and help each other, feeds into this. It just happens that the Outback community is one where they stick together and live under difficult conditions.'

Story Issues

—

'The "help" in each episode, as such, is often very small and unsensational. One was about a wombat who saw that everyone else seemed to have visitors, but no one came to see him, so he invented an invisible friend. While some thought this was a bit silly, the Koala Brothers were very supportive, and asked the wombat and his friend for dinner, and there they encouraged him to invite people over, and they also arranged for all the townsfolk to visit. It is not a big issue, but children see such small things as big in their own lives. Another story was about a cricket match where teams are picked and a penguin is left out. The Koalas bring the penguin in, and everyone realises that it is not nice to feel left out.

'There are running themes, too, about affection, for example, and there is a lot of hugging and physical warmth and supportiveness, which is possible with animal characters, though sometimes more problematic with human characters, especially for American markets. *The Koala Brothers'* world is in the middle of nowhere, but offers the children the possibility that if they went far enough they would encounter this place and community, like in *Pingu*, for example, or most famously, in Lucas's "galaxy, far, far, away". It chimes with the real world, too, in that it is like the Flying Doctor Service and Outback communities pulling together. The message throughout is a positive one.'

10.1

The Koala Brothers – **Dave Johnson**

Frank and Buster, the Koala Brothers, with their friends Ned and Mitzi, are the key characters and central points of empathy for children watching – their appeal lies in their selfless desire to help and care for others. This facilitates much of the action as Frank and Buster fly from one context or situation to another.

The plane is not especially 'modern' and carries with it connotations of being 'personal' to the Koala Brothers in a similar way to Noddy's car; consequently it also embodies the simplicity of traditional children's stories and illustrative concepts.

Here the Brothers share time with their friends around the camp fire, a simple embodiment of community and co-dependence in the face of the limitations of their environment.

The series relies on simple story scenarios where something can go wrong or is needed by a character, and the Koala Brothers help by resolving the issue – here, the beginnings of some problems for Ned on his boat.

11.2

**Stills from Nick Jr. ident –
Michael Frierson**

Frierson's knowledge of cartoon
gags helped him determine
the comic scenario of the
ident. Drawing from historical
precedents and previous work
is an important aspect of
creative work in speaking to the
expectations of the audience,
while also including surprise and
original elements.

Digital Animation

The history of digitally produced animation begins outside the sphere of the entertainment industry, emerging out of the work of military and industrial research teams seeking to use computer graphics for the purposes of simulation and technical instruction. The ENIAC (Electronic Numerical Integrator and Computer), created by the US Army at the University of Pennsylvania in 1946, can claim to be the world's first electronic programmable computer and, though a vast contraption, it had little processing power. With the first silicon transistors made in 1954 and integrated circuits in 1958, computers became more powerful and their uses more various, but they were still largely untouched by creative endeavours.

John Whitney was a pioneer in this respect, establishing Motion Graphics Inc. and making analogue computer-generated light effects. He inspired his son, John Whitney Jr., who, in turn, was aware of the more commercially orientated innovation prompted by Ivan Sutherland, with the invention of the 'Sketchpad' in 1962. This device enabled 'drawing with light' into the computer and underpinned the establishment of Evans & Sutherland as the first company to promote computer graphics as a creative technology. Whitney Jr. worked for the company for a short period before joining Information International Inc. (Triple I), specialising in 3D CG simulations. By 1964 when the first digital film recorder became available, John Stehura had made Cibernetik 5.3 using only punch cards and tape, imagining his abstract, computer motion picture in his mind and only seeing its outcome on screen for the first time when using the recorder at General Dynamics in San Diego, USA.

Having worked on an analogue video graphic system for his projects in the early 1970s, Ed Emshwiller made the pioneering *Sunstone* (1979) – a three-minute 3D computer graphic work using traditional frame-by-frame transitions and the use of colour in motion to create movement in static images – which preceded the development of any software or hardware to more easily facilitate such work. Another pioneer, Larry Cuba, made *First Fig* in 1974, and later worked with John Whitney Sr. on *Arabesque* (1975), each effectively working not merely as an experimental film, but as an act of research in the relationship between geometry, mathematics and graphics as they could be expressed through the computer.

One of the most crucial developments in the field, however, was George Lucas's creation of the initial teams that were later to become the nucleus of Industrial Light and Magic (hereafter ILM) and PIXAR – a company later created by Steve Jobs, the founder of Apple Computers, following the purchase of Lucasfilm's Computer Research and Development Division in 1985.

such features, using the available range of computer software packages to create more individual work.

It is clear that as different software packages become more affordable and user friendly, and the use of the computer as a creative tool becomes both a domestic and industrial orthodoxy, the same degree of breadth and variety that has characterised all other approaches and techniques will characterise computer-generated imagery. In many senses, in the same way as the term 'new media' now seems redundant, it is possible that 'CGI' will also become part of a taken-for-granted lexicon of creative practice in animation.

12.2

***Terminator 2: Judgment Day* – James Cameron**

James Cameron uses CGI effectively as a core aspect of the narrative, simultaneously creating the TS cyborg as a character and an effect.

12.3

***The Last Starfighter* – Nick Castle**

Self-consciously playing on the boom in video games and the popularity of *Star Wars*, considerable investment was made in computer-generated effects for the first time.

Animation for Games: Final Fantasies

—

Computer games are phenomenally popular and with each new technological development comes increasingly sophisticated animation. Film and television have been the traditional places that animators have found work, but in recent years the demand for animators in computer games design has been increasing as games become more sophisticated. As narrative and character play more important roles in games, approaches in design and the specificity of the choreography are drawing upon traditional animation. The skill set for games animation is similar to film and TV animation, but there are some important differences.

Media Molecule is a company based in Guildford in the UK who make creative videogames including *LittleBigPlanet* and *Tearaway*. Lluis Danti is an animator there who describes his role as 'in charge of breathing life and personality into the characters that populate our worlds'.

There are many transferable skills that traditionally trained animators have which are useful to computer games design and development. According to Danti, an animator is someone who is able to tell stories that an audience can empathise with. 'This skill is highly transferable not only in game design but in many other aspects of creative media and life.' Indeed, he says that he actually prefers animators who come to

games from film and TV, since their animation skills are better honed. 'The downside is that they require more adaptation time to the games pipeline, but the animation tools for videogames are easy to learn. What is hard is to be a good animator.'

Character animation in games differs from character animation in film or television in the amount of iteration that games require. Danti explains, 'Usually in films, they hand you a storyboard or an animatic where everything is super defined: cameras, duration, layout etc., so you as an animator know exactly what to do. In games, the animation is always at the service of the gameplay. In traditional animation, when you animate a jump, you need to anticipate that moment to make it readable. With videogames, the anticipation is sometimes skipped for gameplay reasons. For example, the most important thing is not to be able to read the movement of the character properly, but to be able to dodge the big fat alien that is about to eat your brains! That's what we call responsiveness.'

12.4 (pp. 156–8)

Tearaway – Lluis Danti

Lluis broke down the development of the main character from *Tearaway*, Iota. *Tearaway* takes place in a world made of paper, so internal logic dictated that their protagonist would be constructed from paper too. Some of the initial designs are shown here.

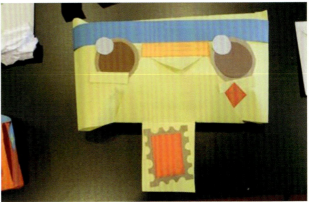

Lluis explained, 'At that time s/he was called Oola, and although it's a very cute character, after some animation tests, we discovered that it was actually kind of difficult for him/her to do very basic actions such as grab objects or run due to their boxy anatomy, so we kept looking for new designs.

It may not look like much, but the important bit at this stage was that we decided our character would have an envelope as a head. So we decided to take this idea and polish it a bit more.'

'We still needed to define how the rest of the body would look, and it was here where our artist, Francis Pang, one of the principle creators of Sackboy from *LittleBigPlanet*, came in with these amazing concepts.'

'That was it, a character that is made of paper, who has an envelope for a head but which has been built around a humanoid body that lets them do all sorts of actions. We finally made it, we just found our heroes: Iota & Atoi!'

Iota and Atoi.

So what qualities is a company like Media Molecule looking for when they recruit animators for games? 'People who are really skilled in keyframe animation, who can create unique animations with a great sense of timing,' says Danti. 'Due to the nature of our games, we don't work with realism so we prefer snappy animations which are closer to a more cartoony style. We prefer candidates with some videogame experience, but the most important thing is to be a GOOD animator.'

In a show reel from a prospective animator Danti is looking for proof that the animator can handle full body acting, as well as 'a close-up shot focusing on facial animation, an action shot with two characters and maybe some creature work. The reel has to be short (below 2 min.) and needs to have the best work at the beginning.'

There is more crossover between games and animation, because of the overlapping skill set required for both. Danti agrees: 'I'm the living example that there is! I've been working in films for six years and it's been two years now that I've been doing games at Media Molecule. Since the quality of videogames is closer to film each time, the industry requires professionals that can handle that level of expectation, which would explain why this crossover is increasing.'

Computer-generated Animation

—

Computer-generated animation has changed the nature of animation as a form and become the dominant approach in TV and feature work. It has prompted a necessary shift in the definition of animation as a model of film-making made frame by frame, or by more synaesthetic means, to incorporate the idea of the conscious manipulation of profilmically constructed synthetic forms in a digital environment. While there is still a fundamental relationship to traditional animation skills and techniques, the software for computer-generated work has changed the nature of the approach.

John Lasseter from PIXAR Animation suggests that there are four key lessons in computer animation:

- The computer is just a tool.
- You cannot tell what it looks like until it is done.
- You get nothing for free.
- You don't get multiple 'takes'.

Lesson 1 – *The computer is just a tool.* We don't like the term 'computer-generated imagery' (CGI), because that gives the feeling that it is the computer that generates or makes the images, and all through my career it has been assumed that the computer does a lot more than it actually does. We all know the difference between a word processor and a typewriter – the word processor doesn't write the stories or articles; cameras don't take photographs. Artists do.

Lesson 2 – *You cannot tell what it looks like until it is done.* People from the advertising industry always want to come out and 'look down the camera' to see how it is going to look, or go to the set or something and it was very hard to tell them that with computer animation you always have to visualise it in your head and have a vision of the finished product – it is one of the key jobs of the director to know that throughout the production. Hence, it is also exciting to work with this technology because of that, because you are excited at every stage of production as it starts to come together.

Lesson 3 – *You get nothing for free.* When you watch any aspect of a computer-animated film, remember one thing: unlike live action, where you can point a camera at the city and start filming, whenever you see a shot in computer animation, every single item that you see on the screen has to be created in the computer. Typically, computers like to make things that are absolutely perfect and clean and sterile-looking, so in our work we are striving to give these worlds a sense of history, a sense of being lived in and that takes a tremendous amount of effort and man hours to be able to do.

Lesson 4 – *You don't get multiple takes.* For those that work in live action, you get to the sound stage or the location and you get to shoot the scene from a number of different angles, and then get to do a number of different takes of each of those angles. You have coverage. You can take all that film into the editing room and create the film from all these choices. In animation it is so incredibly expensive to produce an animation shot, we get one chance and one chance alone, so we have to plan everything out in advance by using story reels. You have to plan it out in advance.[1]

12.5
Still from Animex 2005 ident – Seed Animation

NOTE
1. Quoted in the PIXAR Animation Masterclass, London Film Festival, National Film Theatre, November 2001.

CGI Independent Studio Work
—

Computer-generated 3D animation is still the dominant aesthetic in Hollywood feature animation, thanks to the continuing success of films such as *Frozen* and the *Toy Story* franchise. The use of comparatively affordable software packages that can be used on a domestic computer, and the increase of university and college courses that now teach computer-generated animation has led to a proliferation of these skills, but it is really in the work of independent studios that ground-breaking work has been done in this area.

STUDIO AKA is a small animation production company based in London and acknowledged worldwide for its innovative and idiosyncratic approach to 3D computer-generated animation. They are probably best known for their Lloyds TSB series of bank adverts, and the half-hour short, *Lost and Found* (2008), which has won 61 international awards including a BAFTA for Best Children's Animation.

Director Philip Hunt began his studies in graphic design before studying animation at the Royal College of Art. He worked in Germany and the USA as a stop-motion animator before returning to London and becoming a director at what was to become STUDIO AKA. The company is now co-owned by creative director Hunt alongside senior director Marc Craste and managing director and senior producer Sue Goffe. They employ around 50 people in a tightly knit team that includes directors, producers, digital designers, animators and technical artists,

Philip Hunt describes his transition from working in stop-motion to CGI:

Hunt: 'As a one time diehard stop-motion geek, I did not look twice at digital until two things happened to change my interest and direction. The first was when the feature film I was hired to work on in the States was switched from a stop-motion to CGI production and I was suddenly out of work – and the second was when I saw *Toy Story* for the first time and realised that the possibilities of the digital realm had just been blown wide open. So although I tend to be first and foremost a designer and maker, it was suddenly apparent that CGI seemed to present a limitless palette and toolbox by which to create whatever I could imagine. I've not lost my love of stop-motion but overall I'd have to say that my design background is something that keeps me interested in working in as many different styles as I can muster, and aside from the astonishing amount of writing I seem to do these days, digital allows me an amazing creative visual freedom.'

The tools that STUDIO AKA use to animate with are a mixture of analogue and digital: 'Pencils, paper, Photoshop, Flash, After Effects and Maya. We use a number of different render processes and our main objective is to always let the project dictate the toolset – never the other way around. The old expression "to cut one's cloth accordingly" sums this approach up perfectly. The tools we apply to a job are defined by the creative intent working within the constraints of available time and budget – and as such, things vary accordingly.

'Every technique has its foibles and idiosyncrasies – but mostly it's all about organising people across their roles in the production crew. We work around the complexity of the idea and its execution, and sometimes the simplest projects can end up being the most technically demanding. But if you focus yourself on the organisation of your team and workflow, you free up the process to allow for some really interesting visual expression.'

The film *Lost and Found* came about by chance:

Hunt: 'We were approached by the film's executive producer Joan Lofts, who had secured the rights to the book by Oliver Jeffers. We came on board as co-production partners because it was suddenly clear to us that we wanted to create a film aimed at children, and Oliver's book was the perfect project to take on. We adapted the original story and content to suit both the 30-minute time slot and our desire to present the story in a way that acknowledged the shift from print to screen, and the narrative possibilities that were presented. The single greatest contribution was that of Oliver who was fearless in allowing us to adapt, change and generally mess with his creation.

'The deadline did not allow for us to ponder or experiment, we jumped straight in and the main writing and boarding were completed within a couple of months. The pipeline allowed for the sets and props to be built along the way as needed, and even though principal animation started quite early on, it was often working within still undefined spaces or, in the case of our eventual water simulation – without an ocean! We kept things very simple, swapping out the animatic frames with blocked scenes, animation, and finally rendered shots as we went along. The soundtrack came together towards the end, working to a set timeline so that we brought all the final elements of the film into place during the last few weeks of production. Spreading out the lighting and texture work so that it did not bottleneck at the production end was crucial, and the production overview was kept tightly organised so that we targeted all the hours we had and made as efficient a use of the crew as was possible. In the end the team all went the extra mile to resolve a few last-minute hitches and we hit our deadline with some hours to spare.'

12.6

Stills from the film *Lost and Found* – Philip Hunt

Philip explained, 'The whole film was created on an impossible schedule – we delivered it inside 11 months – and serves as an example of what can be achieved when all the principal creators are working in harmony towards a fully understood goal.'

Philip Hunt's advice to people wanting to enter the 3D CGI animation sector is as follows:

- 'Don't get too hung up on deciding which sector of the industry you want to work in too soon – don't let the goal of a specific skill set cloud the importance of keeping yourself adaptable and open to new opportunities.

- 'Focus on the core skills of drawing and making, don't forget to read and learn to love writing. Keep a sketchbook and add something new every day (believe me, once you stop it's very hard to start again) and scour the great resources on the Internet for supplementary education. Learn your craft, learn its history, then go out and add your unique voice.

- 'The way into any studio seems to naturally polarise between being a generalist and a specialist – but it's the generalists who have more options down the line.

- 'New software will always replace that which you've just begun to master, so make your self adaptable to, and conversant with, the latest developments as they appear – but don't forget that what a good studio looks for most of all is a communicable team player who demonstrates creative talent and an ability to work beyond just what the software can do out of the box.

- 'Don't rely on anything other than the core skills of drawing and designing as they will transcend any digital production package – and so will you.

- 'We have learnt solely from trial and error and the accumulated experience that results. We are a creatively diverse group of artists who often work in close collaboration with each other and the interesting people we meet as part of that process. We aim to create work that will last and we have built a studio by finding ways to make that happen. Much of what we do is work related to a project's journey and not its final destination, ideas we discard, concepts which are set aside, and work which is just lost along the way. The only good advice anyone will give you is to push yourself to be the best at whatever you love, and in the end, talent will always find its way.'

An Unusual Use of CGI

—

As in any kind of artistic endeavour, it is usually the more maverick, independent spirits who progress the form beyond its mainstream incarnation. Those artists in animation who explore the codes, conventions, history and preoccupations of the form have a rich vocabulary from which to draw and a language that permits them to originate new work. Chris Landreth wanted to make a film that, while being a personal statement, was nevertheless profoundly related to the animation community and sought to progress the form.

Ryan, directed by Chris Landreth, is one of computer animation's most celebrated short films in that it displays extraordinary technique in telling a story that is close to the heart of the animation community. Part documentary, part traditional animation, part nightmare, the film is about Ryan Larkin, a Canadian animator, who during the 1960s made *Cityscape* (1963), *Syrinx* (1964) and *Walking* (1969), three celebrated films at the National Film Board of Canada, but who now lives on welfare and begs for change on Montreal streets.

Landreth adopts an approach called 'psychological realism', which uses the fluid language of animation to embrace the concept defined by writer Anaïs Nin when she suggested: 'We don't see things as they are. We see things as we are.' Though using Larkin's voice and those of colleagues and friends, the characters on screen are entirely 'subjective', sometimes fragmented, distorted, or in some way unusual.

12.7

Stills from *Ryan* – Chris Landreth

Influenced by the confluence of realistic facial and bodily representation, and the sense of the grotesque in works by artists as various as Francis Bacon, Ivan Albright and Andrzej Pagowski, Chris Landreth's *Ryan* simultaneously depicts interior and exterior states, redefining the parameters of 'documentary' and the relationship between animation and 'live action'.

Art and technology: Ryan

—

Landreth studied theoretical, applied and fluid mechanics at Master's and research level at the University of Illinois before joining Alias | Wavefront in 1994 testing animation software. He made two well-received films, *The End* (1995) and *Bingo* (1998), the latter being an adaptation of a live theatre performance called *Disregard This Play* by the Chicago-based theatre company The Neo-Futurists.

Ryan sometimes appears as if it is modified 'live action', but everything was conceived and executed in the computer and all character movement was created by hand and did not use motion capture. The film used Alias's Maya animation software (V 4.0) for modelling, rigging, animation, lighting and rendering of the 3D environment, and Discreet Combustion V2.1 for all compositing and 2D effects. Adobe Photoshop V7.0 was employed for painting and texturing, and Adobe Premiere for creative development and editing.

Digital Effects and 3D Animation

—

3D digital effects are now the staple ingredient of Hollywood movies, present in every blockbuster and genre film. However, an undervalued aspect of contemporary 3D computer-generated animation is the work undertaken for television programmes and graphic inserts. In many ways, this has become a necessary area of research, development and progress in television because the viewing audience has been schooled in the 'state-of-the-art' look of contemporary film. Simply, audiences now expect better effects, even on TV, where budgets, of course, are significantly lower. Invention, therefore, has to be greater.

Andy McNamara and his colleagues in the BBC Digital Effects and 3D Animation unit execute a variety of material from the CBeebies and BBC 2 idents to more

involved work like that undertaken for CBBC Scotland's *Shoebox Zoo*, a 13-part series written by Brian Ward.

Aesthetic consistency

—

Paul Kavanagh worked on the character design and graphics for *Shoebox Zoo*, liaising with Claire Mundell, head of BBC Scotland, production designer, Tom Sayer, and costume designer, Ali Mitchell, to achieve an aesthetic consistency in the work, drawing upon design sources in Celtic mythology. The production was achieved in collaboration with Calibre Digital Pictures in Toronto, Canada, who were responsible for the principal animation.

The story

—

The story begins with Marnie McBride's eleventh birthday, a low-key affair coming so soon after her mother's death and her displacement from her home in Colorado to Scotland. A passing visit to a junk shop results, however, in Marnie finding a shoebox containing four animal figures – Edwin the Eagle (Rik Mayall), Bruno the Bear (Alan Cumming), Wolfgang the Wolf (Simon Callow) and Ailsa the Adder (Siobhan Redmond) – which eventually come to life and lead her into an unexpected adventure where she must encounter Toledo the shapeshifter, and discover the secrets of the Book of Forbidden Knowledge, written by one Michael Scot. Such stories often rest on the capacity for transformation and metamorphosis, as well as the creation of fantastical forms and contexts, and this is intrinsically related to the vocabulary of animation to facilitate such work.

Plausible reality

—

This 3D computer-generated imagery is a crucial factor in facilitating the 'fantasy' of the story, but it must also aspire to a plausible reality if the fantasy is to sustain itself as a believable narrative. The animation here does not merely authenticate the narrative, but enables the design sources to reinforce the mythological aspects of the adventure in an accessible and engaging way.

Design for purpose

This kind of work echoes the commercial sector in the sense that animators and effects practitioners must respond efficiently and sensitively to a brief, and the broadcast context. It is crucial that design both facilitates aesthetic needs and also works as a persuasive animated effect.

a

12.8

Progression from original sketch to composited, animated character, from *Shoebox Zoo* – Andy McNamara

The first image (a) shows one of the original sketches for Wolfgang the Wolf, based on the richly decorative animal carvings of the Celtic period. While being 'authentic' in echoing the entwined forms of the relief carving characteristic to these artefacts, this also posed potential problems for the animation of the figures, and the visual appeal of the animals to an audience predominantly made up of children.

b

The animals' figures had to work both as artefacts in their own right and as manipulable figures in computer imagery. Consequently, the figures had to work as though they were made out of metal, stone and wood, yet also move in a way that enabled convincing animated action while retaining the characteristics and properties of these materials. The first CG maquette (b) seeks to address this issue and provide the 'frozen' sleeping position of the character before it comes to life.

c

Shoebox Zoo required that each animal figure become an actual prop, so the initial 'rig' of the frozen Wolfgang was sent to Arrk, a stereo lithographic company specialising in creating resin maquettes (c).

d

Kavanagh worked with Calibre's Jean Jacques Chaboissier on the texturing of the maquettes. The maquette of Wolfgang becomes both a functional prop for the live action sequences and a model for computer-generated extrapolation (d).

e

As well as resembling an ancient artefact, the character also had to appeal as a toy. This necessitated research in the now defunct Pollocks' toy museum in London. Wolfgang is shown as a fully textured computer-generated form (e), now able to move from the 'frozen' initial rig, to a range of 'performance' positions.

f

g

All of the CG work in *Shoebox Zoo* was conducted in Maya, but compositing – the mapping of Wolfgang into the desired physical environment – was achieved using Discreet's Combustion package (f, g). The CG character interacts with the live-action characters and environment; the lighting a key aspect in creating the shadow that enhances the three-dimensional presence of an imaginary, mythic, illusionary figure as a 'real' character in an actual environment.

12.9

The other *Shoebox Zoo* characters

The other characters are Ailsa the Adder, Bruno the Bear, and Edwin the Eagle.

Rotoscope and Motion Capture

—

The role of rotoscoping in animated film demonstrates the most self-evident place where live action and animation meet. Mark Langer defines the rotoscope as: 'A device that allowed the rear projection of a live-action film frame-by-frame on to a translucent surface set into a drawing board. An animator could simply trace each live-action image on to a piece of paper, advance the film by another frame and repeat the process. By these means, the live-action images became a guide to detailed and life-like animation.'[2]

The Fleischer Brothers, for example, rotoscoped the distinctive loping 'dance-walk' of singer Cab Calloway for their cartoon shorts, *Minnie the Moocher* (1932), in which he becomes a ghost walrus, and *Snow White* (1933), where he doubles for Koko the clown, his body at one point changing into a liquor bottle. Disney famously used the process for the human figures in *Snow White and the Seven Dwarfs* (1937). Ralph Bakshi also employed the technique in his epics, *Wizards* (20th Century Fox, 1977) and *The Lord of the Rings* (1978), but for the most part the technique has often been viewed as 'inauthentic' in some way.

Disney veteran Ollie Johnston, one of the true 'greats' in the development of traditional animation, suggests: 'At Disney we used film to study the movement and when we used the rotoscope, we made Photostats of each frame of action so we could trace the movements for an animated sequence. But we noticed something. We saw that film gave us every single movement and tracing it meant that the human body became kind of stiff, and didn't move like a person at all. Film gave us too much information, so we had to emphasise what was important to the animator – the squash 'n' stretch movement of a figure, the anticipation, the overlapping action – and act through the movement, so that you choose what you want to exaggerate to get the right action for the scene and no more.'[3]

From a different perspective, Johnston stresses the limits of live action. The animator must be selective in the choice of what the animated figure needs to do in relation to the requirements of the scene. The movement is not about capturing the physical wholeness of a body, but the specific imperatives that create an action. This is further related to the weight of the figure, the kind of movement through space and time, the sense of rhythm, adaptation to the environment, effort needed and gestural specificity. This is clearly related to aspects of the 'performance' of the animated character as it is determined by the animator as 'actor'. This sense of 'performance' has become intrinsically related to the use of 'motion capture' in more recent work.

NOTES

2. M. Langer, 'The Fleischer Rotoscope Patent', *Animation Journal*, 1.
3. Interview with Paul Wells, April 1999.

Remembering key movement issues

Rotoscoping and motion capture may be viewed as helpful tools in the development of animated movement, but it still remains the case that all 'movement', however ultimately constructed or presented, must be motivated, and that movement is still informed by overlapping action, distortion, forced perspective, motion blur, and any number of performative 'takes' and 'gestures' to signal particular meanings.

12.10

First draft maquettes and the final monster designs for *Oby* **– Anja Perl and Max Stolzenberg**

Students Perl and Stolzenberg worked on various designs for their monster (top left) before settling on the final one (top right). This became the working template for the model sheet. Once the maquette design was decided upon (bottom right), it was transferred to computer for digital modelling (bottom left).

Matt Ferro, visual effects supervisor for *The Matrix* (Warner Bros., 1999), while championing the possibilities of 'motion capture' – literally, attaching sensors to a real moving body as reference points for data transferred into the computer to facilitate digitally constructed figures – nevertheless harbours anxiety about the ways in which this supposedly creates 'realism' in the movement of animated characters. He says: 'This stylised naturalism, which is rendered so photo-realistically, and which takes the depiction of violence seriously [in work like *Roughnecks: Starship Troopers Chronicles*, 2000] and not cartoonally, speaks more directly to games fans', adding, 'we need to look at the subtextual meaning of movement under these circumstances, especially as kids under ten can see this stuff at 8.00 a.m. in the morning all over the world'.[4]

Ferro's key point here about the 'subtextual meaning of movement' in many ways reinforces the point made by Johnston and remains a crucial observation for animators, whatever technology or approach they are using. What remains vital is the authenticity that traditional animation techniques and motion capture can bring to the distinctive 'world' imagined by the animator within the context of the narrative or set of story events.

Motion capture has progressed considerably in recent years and, allied to sophisticated CGI and the more self-conscious imperatives of actors working through motion capture equipment, this has created work of a progressive nature, most notably in the case of Andy Serkis's truly immersed performance as Gollum in Peter Jackson's *The Lord of the Rings: The Two Towers* (2002).

Serkis drew on sources as various as Caliban in Shakespeare's *The Tempest*, Victor Hugo's *Hunchback of Notre Dame*, Robert Louis *Stevenson's Dr Jekyll and Mr Hyde*, and works by Otto Dix, Francis Bacon and Brom, in the creation of a character that he had

to play as a reference guide for other actors, in real-time motion capture for CGI data, as an 'automated dialogue replacement', creating audio tracks for the character, and as a moving template for the animation process itself.[5]

A combination of processes was used in the construction of Gollum's action: traditional rotoscoping, where fight sequences conducted by Serkis were recorded and his movement drawn over frame by frame to ensure Gollum fought with the high degree of energy and aggression required; key frame animation (this was used for action that would be impossible for a human actor to perform); and most particularly, the face, and motion capture, where much of Serkis's performance dictated Gollum's on-screen activity.

At the heart of this, once more, was the persuasiveness of Gollum as a character in his own right, where the animation facilitates the character and, in this instance, necessarily has to efface the performance of the actor, but must not draw attention to itself as animation, or as an effect. A key point to emerge from all of this is that animation almost intrinsically hides its process, and the 'art' that characterises that process, but it is the final outcome that justifies this necessity.

NOTES

4. Interview with Paul Wells, November 2000.
5. All the material here concerning Gollum is drawn from A. Serkis, *The Lord of the Rings: Gollum* (Boston and New York, Houghton Mifflin Company, 2003).

Combining Live Action and Animation Using Motion Capture for CGI

—

Working with motion capture can be helpful for facilitating a particular kind of motion in computer-generated figures, sometimes in a spirit more closely echoing the dynamics of live-action characters that may be in the same environment. Compositing – literally bringing together layers of pictorial elements to create an image – can seamlessly enable live-action characters and environments to coexist with animated characters and objects in a visual space, informed by the same movement characteristics.

Anja Perl and Max Stolzenberg, students of the Filmakademie, Ludwigsberg, Baden's Institute for Animation, Visual Effects and Digital Postproduction, sought in their film *Oby* to combine live action and animation by creating a 3D CGI monster, Oby, and have him have a human encounter with a lady making pancakes.

Oby, while being created in Maya, also benefited from 'motion capture' using Motionbuilder, which required a human actor to perform so as to generate some of Oby's movements.

Perl: 'The challenge was the motion capture for CGI because we hadn't done that before. A professional dancer and I mimed the dance of the monster, which was quite an experience, and later on I was cleaning up the MoCap-data and doing additional animation with a program I had to learn within two weeks, while Max was modelling, lighting, texturing, rendering and compositing the scenes. We had a few fantastic people around us helping, and fortunately we had no major problems in the working process. Maybe we were very lucky, but we had tried to plan a project that is manageable for the two of us and a small crew in a working period of three months. Crucially, Max and I are pretty good in work sharing.'

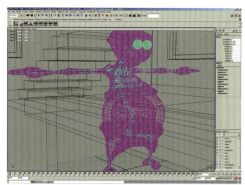

12.11

Production reference and screengrabs from *Oby* – Anja Perl and Max Stolzenberg

Real-world objects were used to give the monster's skin a realistic surface. Images of these objects were scanned and texture-mapped on to the three-dimensionally rendered character using a computer. Layers of texture were carefully built up for a convincing appearance.

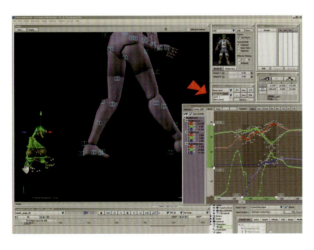

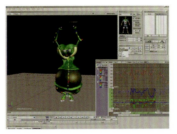

12.12

Production photos and screengrabs from *Oby*

The motion capture process involves attaching sensors to human performers as they play out the physical sequences that make up the animation (top images); in this case, Oby's dance is enacted. Using Maya 5.0, the data captured from the performance of Oby's dance is then transferred from the human form on to the fictional monster's form (bottom images).

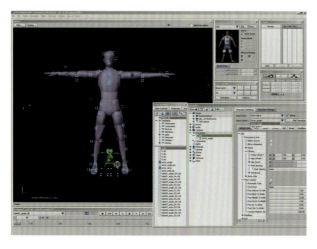

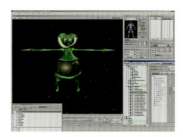

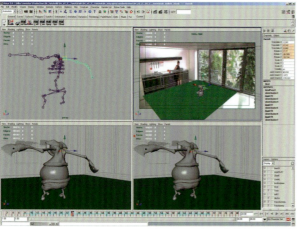

12.13

Screengrabs from *Oby*

Once the character has been animated using the motion capture data in Maya 5.0, the digitised model is then exported into Motion Builder software, in order to add characterisation.

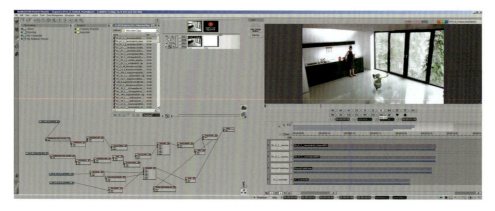

12.14

Stills from *Oby*

The final stage in this digital animation was compositing the character into the intended context of a kitchen. Lighting was added to the figure to correspond with the light sources in the kitchen – the bank of windows – and helped create the sense of the character really existing within the space left and below.

Perl and Stolzenberg take the fantasy creature into the everyday, but simultaneously into an avant-garde model of narrative and visual presentation.

The pipeline: from conception to completion

—

Zourelidi: 'We have a script editor and a team of writers that pitch story ideas and write the scripts. The supervising director and the episode directors go through the story outlines and scripts and send their feedback. Rovio's CEO Mikael Hed reviews the episodes at key stages of production and gives his feedback.

'Once the script is locked the episode director briefs the concept artist for any locations, props or costumes that might be needed. Once those are finalised the director briefs the story artist. The story artist first creates thumbnails and pitches those to the director. Following this the story artist draws the panels. After the first pass the boards go to the editor, who edits them into an animatic. The director records a temp track with all the characters' voices to help tell the story. There are several reviews with the director, story artist and editor as well as the supervising director.

'Once the animatic is locked the final voices are recorded with the actors and the sound designer edits a temp sound track for animation.

'The backgrounds and props are designed based on the concept art created earlier and are adapted if there are any changes in the animatic. The layout begins as well as the colour script created.

'After layout the director briefs the animation supervisor. Together they go through in detail every shot. Usually the director and animation supervisor shoot a live action video ref, acting out key moments of the story. In parallel The FX department creates visual references or keys for the FXs that will need to be animated. The animation supervisor writes the animation brief shot by shot, explaining in detail what is required from the animators. He/she will also write a brief for any FXs in the episode. There are several rounds of animation and the director is present on key rounds. After each round the shots go back to the editor who checks the cuts, as well as the overall edit of the episode.

'Once the character animation is locked in rough animation, the FX animation begins. The character animation then goes through clean-up and colour. At the same time the background colour artists are painting the backgrounds.

'Once animation, FX and BG work is complete the episode goes to the compositing team. The director and supervising compositing artist go through the episode shot by shot.

'At the final stages of compositing, the episode goes to editorial for a final time lock. This is when the episode is edited to the correct length. Once the picture is locked the director briefs the sound designer and music editor. The music editor works with the composers on the score and Foley sound is recorded.

'Finally the episode goes to sound mix and colour grade. In colour grade the colours and tones are checked and adjusted to make sure the episode will look its best on the various devices and monitors. The title cards are created and the episode is ready to be aired.'

Zourelidi's advice to people wanting to work in this section of the industry is simple: 'Draw, draw, draw! Life drawing, caricatures, expressions; anything and everything to help you develop your technical and observational skills. Practise drawing strong and extreme poses – don't worry about messy drawings; the most important thing is to capture the movement and the essence of your characters.

'When animating a character don't just do a generic walk cycle; think about their personalities and how does this affect their movements,' she advises.

'Some of the best animators that I have worked with are the ones that *own* the shots/scenes that they are working with. When you are animating a shot think about where this sits in the bigger picture of the film/episode. What was your character doing before this moment and what will happen afterwards? Think about the continuity of the shots and how the movement will cut.'

Communication is crucial when working on a larger production. 'If someone else is animating the shot before or after yours, talk to them to see what they are planning to do so that the action picks up from one shot to the next. Work with strong poses first;

think about the key moments in the shot and block those out.'

She also warns students not to be too parochial in their thinking; animation is a global industry and travelling to, and perhaps living in, different countries can be part of the job. 'Remember that your competition is not just your fellow students but people from around the world. Study animation, study film language. Always be a student and strive for your best. Keep at it and never give up!'

The auteur in animation

Live-action cinema has a canon of directors defined by the critical community as 'auteurs' – the presiding authorial voice in a film, or across a number of films, with a recognisable signature style or preoccupying theme. Arguably, though, animation, especially in the context of 'alternative methods', is the most auteurist of media. Often, films are made by one person alone and are expressly dealing with a specific and complex theme, a new technique, or using an experimental approach to a dominant method. Much of the rest of the work in this book has this aspect, either by virtue of extending the parameters of fine art in animation or by using digital technologies and new exhibition opportunities to extend the boundaries of the form.

13.1
Still from *Colour Box* – Len Lye

Len Lye's work in painting, etching and creating colour overlays directly on to the film stock was highly influential as a model of abstract animation, intrinsically informed by spontaneity and intuitive expression.

Fine Art Practices

—

The relationship between fine art and animation practice is in some ways an under-explored aspect of animation, while contradictorily, the very method by which it is often understood as an 'art' in its own right. This is partly because the traditional techniques of fine art practice are seen to be applied in a time-based context and may be evidenced not merely through the process work, but in the final film itself.

Animation is an incredibly plastic medium and the ways to animate are as diverse as the animator's imagination dictates. *Imperial Provisor Frombald* (2013) was a commission by Animate Projects for Channel 4 television's Random Acts series. Director Elizabeth Hobbs created this film by printing rubber stamps directly onto 35 mm film stock and then digitally scanning the printed stock.

13.2
Imperial Provisor Frombald **– Elizabeth Hobbs**
A selection of the rubber stamps made for this film.

A Philosophical Approach

—

Animation has long been regarded as a 'metaphysical' practice, one which by virtue of its technique, in whatever form, necessitates that the animator is self-conscious about the relationship between the 'idea' and the method of its expression, and, for those who teach animation or wish to reach new audiences, how this might be best expressed to students or those with an invested interest. Animation, again especially when played out through 'alternative methods', is very often informed by an exploratory, philosophical sensibility, using the medium to embody a specific view or vision.

Animators like Maureen Selwood and Rachel Bevan Baker, whose views and work appear here, are constantly exploring the relationship between traditional concepts and techniques, and the 'modernity' of the form. This is partly in the desire to extend the artistic parameters of the form, but also to look at the art as a system of ideas. This 'philosophical' approach can then be extended to teaching and alternative forms of exhibition, as well as validating the purpose of the art.

Maureen Selwood is a practising film-maker and tutor at the world-renowned California Institute of the Arts (CalArts). She has a particular interest in the relationship between creative work and teaching, and seeks to articulate the approach to her own work as a starting point for facilitating others.

Selwood: 'My work springs from drawing and the ideas that come from the images I create. I feel drawing is a means of expression that is fresh and vital, especially when the line feels active and engaged. In the beginning I studied the work of artists whose images would be interesting to appreciate for their simplicity yet rich subject matter. Jean Cocteau, Miró and Matisse filled my head with the idea that I could draw from an interior place and still find a structure for ideas.'

Influences

—

'Animation in the beginning was the most exciting form for me to think about these things. My techniques seem to change somewhat with each film, but drawing is always the anchor. I went to film school to study live-action film-making and that period of study has stayed with me in that I still like to marry live footage with animation, but sometimes, too, I like to work with pure drawing. By changing the technique I feel I am in a new place and can move outside myself and have a different take on the place of my story. Writing and drawing share a rather equal relationship. I remember reading about Miró and how he described his process of writing about the drawings and paintings he was going to make. I understood this and found it like animation.'

Experimentation

—

Again, it is important to recognise that this kind of film-making likes to draw upon the 'theorisation' of creative practice as it has been addressed by artists of all kinds. Reading about the ways in which artists think about their work and seek to execute it is fundamental to both establishing a technique and a set of skills, but it also prompts ideas for renewing or extending experimentation in a different form. In the following examples, Selwood stresses her continuing interest in technique, but also the place that her work finds in the active experience of living her life. 'Creativity is fundamentally inspired by remaining conscious of the relationship between methods of expression, knowledge of a range of fine art and popular forms, and the articulation of personal thoughts and feelings at any one period of living.' Selwood has clearly engaged with the animation medium, and in bringing her knowledge of art and personal experience to the work, has been able to make distinctive films. She recognises, however, that the student starting out may not have the confidence to fully embrace the possibilities.

Selwood: 'I think when students first start to draw for animation they aren't sure if they possess their own work yet. Animation can take a long time to feel identified with it. There are many famous names with distinct styles that at first confront the student of animation. It is important to study the form, but it is also important to allow that new voices are crucial in developing it. It can take a unique approach to help students claim this territory. I think it is most helpful for students of animation to give images to the mental processes that move their imagination fairly early on. I believe drawing is the first step towards that. But of course, collage, photography and puppetry are starting points too. Drawing can become a kind of handwriting to realise ideas and narratives.'

13.4

Still from _Hail Mary_ – Maureen Selwood

'_Hail Mary_ gave me an opportunity to write and work from a pre-recorded soundtrack. I wanted the images to be in black and white and I deliberately left out an image of a woman. The story was told through the details and the structure was based on the Catholic rosary, which was fun to play with. The voice-over is rather obsessive and the woman uses numbers every time she describes something. It gave the recording a new kind of rhythm, especially as the actress added more to the obsessive nature of the details.'

13.5

Stills from _Flying Circus_ – Maureen Selwood

'_Flying Circus: An Imagined Memoir_ was made at a time when I wanted to play with colour and how it affects mood. I adapted the opera _Parade_ by Cocteau, Satie and Picasso and used it to instil a memory from childhood that shows the rich healing power of the imagination of a child. I worked with many different colouring methods and time-lapsed painted still photographs.

I thought of the animation as showing the tensions of balance and imbalance for the sense of mood and place inside a circus tent. I loved animating this film. It was liberating, but quite difficult to animate. I worked with other animators for the first time on my own work and found collaboration exciting.'

13.6

Still from *As You Desire Me* – Maureen Selwood

'In *As You Desire Me* I am again marrying drawing to live footage. This piece was inspired by the play by Pirandello and will be three poetic narratives. I am designing more surreal characters here, moving away from the direct figurative style of past work. I lived in Rome for a year and that experience was transformative in my shifting style. I was surrounded every day by art and the sculpture all around Rome of the human figure filled with emotion. I have also begun to create installations for my films and find that the thrilling aspect of this is that it brings new audiences to animation.'

Approaches to teaching

—

Selwood has some approaches to her teaching that seek to liberate them from the constraints that can sometimes be very inhibiting. Students can often not progress their work effectively if their benchmark is the 'full animation' of Disney or PIXAR, or the virtuousity of McLaren, Svankmajer, or Norstein.

Selwood: 'There are also metaphorical concepts that can help a student illustrate an important way to tell a story. The labyrinth, for example, can be an excellent way to open a film about a struggle where a protagonist is fleeing an unsafe place. In this case I will bring to the class a myth associated with the metaphor. I love live-action films where the photography is especially meaningful to me. I find it inspiring and it often will segue into my own dream life of images and stories. Dreams are always a most interesting place not for a fully realised story, but for

moments to let one's imagination picture a scene or idea. I teach drawing workshops for students on surrealism. We study the period of surrealism and appreciate how a painting may be limited, while the time-based aspect of film allows for an arrangement of images over time and thus a more restrained telling, but with a surprising outcome. It can be one that allows the viewer a process to enter into the complexity of the world of the artist. Students love this method. The mix of images they create and how quickly they are able to conceptualise often surprises them. I too find this a rather marvellous method. These same images sometimes gather in a different arrangement allowing for a freedom with storyboarding previously thought to be a difficult process.'

An alternative approach

—

This use of established myths, metaphors, dream imagery and surrealist painting liberates the student from a 'literal' interpretation of the world, a 'realist' approach to representation, and the structural demands of classical narrative. This 'alternative' approach enables students to work creatively in a different way from the methodologies outlined earlier in this book. Crucially, it is enabling in getting students started and points them quickly to the ways in which they would prefer to work, and the type of work they would like to engage in.

Selwood: 'CalArts is a place with many diverse schools of thought throughout, whether it is critical thinking, dance, theatre, music, art or animation. There are always influences. In the Experimental Animation Programme where I teach drawn animation, I fuse experimental techniques with classical skills. But for me the ideas come first. I think if a student has the passion to say something, that will drive the discipline to do it the best way possible. I try to help students warm up to the process of animation. I try to teach about how to make things move in an inspired and engaged way. The old UPA cartoons are just as viable as any current films by important animation artists working today.'

Working process

—

'Computer technology now has a presence not previously thinkable in the beginning of teaching animation. I try to get students as quickly as possible to use the computer so the process of conceptualising isn't foreign to how they will make their projects. I am amazed at what students are able to accomplish and how quickly the learning curve is learned.'

Selwood, like many animation practitioners, seeks to illuminate her own working process by making films about it: 'At the moment I am working on two films: *Drawing Lessons* and *As You Desire Me*. In *Drawing Lessons* I am hoping to make a truly humorous film about the obsessive nature of trying to learn to draw by doing the same exercise over and over again. The mind gets distracted, but the process of drawing continues. I will use an awkward drawing style, but one that is easier to animate to tell the story of a woman obsessed with learning to draw. By shifting the style of the drawing, the process of animating reveals the humour in this struggle.'

13.7

Still from *The Rug* – Maureen Selwood

'*The Rug* is an earlier work in which I adapted a story by the Irish writer Edna O'Brien. This story allowed for me to explore the part of Ireland that my mother came from and imagine aspects of her life through this story. I left Ireland as a young child so I escaped a world I had been born into but really never knew.'

Very much in the spirit of Maureen Selwood, Rachel Bevan Baker seeks to explore through drawing and to find new contexts and audiences for animation. Her work *Beaches* has found a place in a traditional gallery and as live work on the Web. This embrace of tradition and modernity is fundamental to many working in an 'alternative' and more auteurist fashion, but often starts from some basic principles.

Baker: 'I love drawing and always had a very lively free style to my line, so it felt very natural to make my drawings move. It seemed an easy step to take. I like the freedom animation gives – no rules of the real world. I increasingly like the aspect of working with sound – at first I didn't spend much time on soundtracks (limited by knowledge and technology), but now that side of film-making excites me almost more than the drawing. I like the fact that animation can be such a complex process because it forces simplification – it is similar to poetry in that respect, that a short, apparently simple film can be full of ideas and meaning – they can be intense experiences to watch.'

On location
—

Baker's *Beaches* project was funded by a Creative Scotland Award from the Scottish Arts Council, and came as a response to working in a studio context making *The Green Man of Knowledge* at Red Kite with the animation team for the best part of a year, and feeling the need to work with greater personal freedom again, released from the restraints of studio production and delivering to broadcasters.

Baker: 'I wanted drawing to return to the heart of my work again and to work intuitively, away from studio trappings of dope sheets/animatics etc. I wanted to work on location as much as possible – not a tradition of animation!

'I worked around the theme of beaches, to create a series of animated pieces of work, linked by theme, but very varied in approach, subject and technology used. The project also gave me a chance to learn some new software, and use it in a non-commercial way. Some of the films were abstract, some more documentary in style, some worked with soundtracks forming first (collaborating with composer John Harris for two of the 11 films). Some were created completely on location with a digital camera mounted on a tripod; I animated on paper, sand, paint, and on acetate, directly under the camera. I wanted to create very immediate, impressionistic animation, inspired by surroundings and weather, and events taking place around me. I also created animated sketchbooks – all drawn on-site, working in a layout pad from back to front, drawing as quick as possible, creating animation of people, surroundings and events as they happened.'

AUTHOR TIP
Tradition and modernity

Aspirant animators should always embrace 'tradition' – the knowledge and skills learned from past achievements and experience in the field – and 'modernity' – the most up-to-date approaches, technologies of expression, and means to creativity. These are some obvious ways in which this might be done:

- Watch and critically engage with as many animated films of whatever style or era as possible.
- Read as much historical, critical and technical material about animation from a range of disciplines.
- Use trade publishing and the World Wide Web to glean up-to-date information about the field.
- Attend animation lectures, events and festivals.

Technology

—

'I used very immediate technology for some of the films (e.g., *Achmelvich*, *Portmahomack*), to work as spontaneously as possible. I wanted as little technology or studio processes to get between the inspiration and the animation.

'For others (e.g., *Chanonry Point*, *Picking up Stones*) I used Flash. They involved ideas gathered over a longer time and repeated visits to the beaches. The films took a little longer to "form". I also wanted to learn new animation software. As a result these were created a little more "traditionally", working with storyboards, all "back at base" in the Red Kite studio.

'Both *Waiting for Dolphins: Chanonry Point* and *Picking up Stones* are excellent examples of translating directly observed activity, through sketching, into an animated form. The former is entirely composed of watching people at the seashore, looking out at passing boats, skimming stones, picking up shells, taking photos, walking with different gaits and purpose, and reacting to the oncoming waves. The "narrative" here is an act of "capture" – recording the small narratives of people by the sea. *Woman in the Zone*, again using Flash, distils this into a meaningful incident as a woman gazing at her reflection in the sea recalls her childhood games at the sea edge, and picks up a shell as a further "souvenir" of the memory.'

Refining technique

—

'After McLaren, I used the technique of charcoal on paper (using it in the same way as paint on glass, working on one sheet of paper and moving, smudging and removing the charcoal frame by frame), because I'd always wanted to try the technique and these short experimental films gave me the opportunity. As in all creative work, some degree of learning takes place and necessitates doing different things than might have otherwise been anticipated. This can have beneficial rewards, too.

'I was working mostly alone and with no producer – my own choice. It was great to have this freedom, but it was also a bit lonely. So I found I enjoyed the films that did bring me back to the studio and allowed me to gain feedback from colleagues. It was refreshing for Red Kite too, to have me in and out of the studio, creating new work and trying new techniques. I ended up taking the role of producer myself, creating schedules of work, budgeting, setting some "rules" to the structure of the work (how many films, how connected etc.), and organising post-production. This was a learning curve, but very rewarding.'

Animated Documentary

Animation has often played a key part in the construction of documentary film but 'animated documentary' as a term began to be discussed in the late 1990s. Partially through the success of feature films like *Waltz with Bashir* (Artificial Eye, 2008) and *Persepolis* (StudioCanal, 2007) animated documentary has become an accepted subgenre. In animation studies Gunnar Strøm, in a 2005 article,[1] pointed out that animated documentary had been largely overlooked for the past 20 years, but texts like Annabelle Honess Roe's overview of the subject, *Animated Documentary* (2013), have been part of cementing its wider acceptance in the field.[2]

Why Use Animation in the Documentary Genre?

—

Animation can bring a special set of qualities to documentary film-making and the most interesting animated documentaries exploit these qualities. Alys Scott Hawkins and Ellie Land are animators who work primarily in the animated documentary genre; they co-created the blog 'animateddocumentary.com'.

Hawkins feels that what animation can bring to the documentary genre is a personal perspective: 'Subjectivity, irreverence, subversion, simplification. Dreams, memories, the taboo. The opportunity to revisit the past, to present what was not or could not be filmed, to exaggerate or to show a singular viewpoint.'

Hawkins says, 'I came to the genre of independent animation as someone who was fascinated and intrigued by such intense and personal visions, contained in the small package of the short film.' She says that it was often films that took a passionately subjective perspective which she found most compelling. 'Early animadoc films I saw were *A is for Autism*, *His Mother's Voice*, *Daddy's Little Piece of Dresden China*, and *Creature Comforts*, *Going Equipped* and *War Story*.'

Hawkins: 'I don't think I recognised such films as "documentaries" at that point, but I was engaged and drawn in by this work which explored and interpreted the world in such a subjective way.

'When I came to make my own films, it was entirely instinctive to do so in a way that reflected or asked questions of the world around me. My first student film project compared means of attraction and desire in humans and animals using animated sequences in a range of different techniques; my second was an experimental narrative short informed by a series of vox pop interviews with women, asking about the freedoms they have as compared with their mothers' generation.

Notes

1. G. Strøm, 'How Swede It Is …' *fps Magazine*, March 2005 [online]. www.fpsmagazine.com/mag/fps200503lo.pdf#page=13 (accessed 10 November 2015).
2. A. Honess Roe, *Animated Documentary* (London: Palgrave Macmillan, 2013).

14.1

Winsor McCay's 1918 film, *The Sinking of the Lusitania*, was an early example of a film in the animated documentary genre.

'My graduation film *Bun in the Oven* more consciously took a documentary subject – pregnancy and childbirth – but set out to subvert and challenge the conventional presentation of this subject matter, for example in a medicalised and "wholesome" way. Though what animation often does is to create a fantasy world, for me it was always using it to explore and reframe the "real world" which was exciting.

'Ellie Land and I founded the [animated documentary] blog in 2011, acknowledging that there was more and more interest in the genre; that it was becoming more recognisable; and that there was an increasing amount of material online, but no central point from which to access or explore it. The time seemed ripe to create a meeting place for film-makers and fans alike, added to which – as what I would describe as confirmed animated documentary directors – we wanted to position ourselves at the centre of that, in order to help make our own work visible.

'Our approach with the blog has always been to build a searchable database of films available online, rather than to curate a selection of recommendations. Alongside the films we share news about funding, festivals, workshops, publications, and we have additional categories for interactive docs and non-fiction graphic novels – separate genres that we consider relevant enough to our readers.'

Hawkins thinks that the growth in interest in animated documentary has come from reaching a critical mass in the work being produced: 'there have been the big releases which have brought the form to a wider audience: *Waltz with Bashir*, *Persepolis* … then there's the growth of documentary features getting cinematic release and TV broadcast which have increasingly featured animated sequences, and in doing so opened up audiences' minds to animation as a tool within documentary [such as *The Age of Stupid*, (Dogwoof, 2008)]. I would say that some of that openness also comes from the availability of short films to watch online. There are big audiences watching a diverse range of short film content, which would previously be extremely hard to access outside of film festivals.'

Co-author of this book and animation director Samantha Moore also works within the animated documentary genre. She says that animated documentary 'has increasingly taken me to the area of working with scientists and collaborators to communicate internal or invisible processes, like the 2010 film *An Eyeful of Sound* which evokes the experience of people who have audio–visual synaesthesia. Synaesthesia is a brain state where, when one sense is stimulated, more than one sense reacts. People who have audio–visual synaesthesia can see as well as hear sounds and music. When I began the project (funded by the Wellcome Trust) it soon became clear that animation was an incredibly effective way to communicate audio-visual synaesthesia to a wider non-synaesthetic audience, because we could actually show them what a synaesthetic person *saw* when listening to a sound.'

Moore, in common with many animated documentary makers, used documentary interviews as the basis for her film but she does not see the sound as being the only (or even a vital) documentary link. 'The interviews we did for the film were recorded but only a fraction of the sound was used. Most of the interviews were used to capture the subject's description of their unique perspective in conjunction with drawing and painting. I would take their paintings and the recordings of their descriptions away to animate digitally, and then send them links to the animated version of their depiction. Many times it was wrong, and I would need to change what I had done to better reflect their internal view. In that slow and collaborative way we eventually reached an animated version, which, according to them, best approximated the experience of having audio-visual synaesthesia. The whole project took three years to complete!'

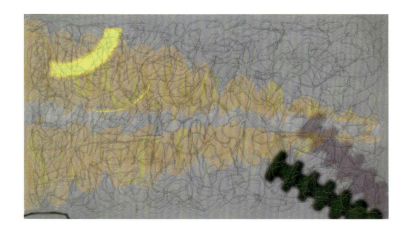

14.2

Stills from *An Eyeful of Sound* – Samantha Moore

This is a film about audio–visual synaesthesia from the perspective of three people who have that brain trait and the scientist who is studying them.

PART

Dandelion.

Poppy.

Contexts

The first two sections of this book have been concerned with the pre-production and production processes of making an animated film, of whatever technique, principle or approach. This final section looks at the latter stages of completing a production and some of the ways in which a piece of work might be a vehicle for finding future employment or training opportunities; the target audience a piece of work might be appropriate for; and the contexts in which an animator might seek to develop a career. This section also provides information for further reading and study. Investment in the field is absolutely vital, and consistently thinking about what can be achieved intellectually, creatively and technically is essential. Constantly pursuing resources to facilitate that process is fundamental to development and eventual success.

Walsh (cont.): 'Technically speaking, special effects perform certain important functions in a classically animated feature film:

- They can serve to heighten the dramatic tension of a scene or exemplify the characters' mood by an effective use of lighting, or detailing other climatic conditions.

- They can also perform a climactic event, which releases the dramatic tension of a sequence, usually in the form of an explosion or a cataclysmic natural disaster.

- They can assist in establishing a sense of environment and give the characters a greater sense of presence in that environment.

- The effects layer also bridges the gap between character and background, and, as the final layer of drawing produced for the scene, it helps to homogenise the different elements into a final cohesive image.

'Commercial narrative conventions demand a number of effects-heavy sequences to punctuate the dramatic development of a story. A good effect is always one that supports the character action and serves its purpose in the development of the narrative. This means that a good effect does not necessarily reside in the largest, most dramatic on-screen moment, but is more often in the subtle detail that is taken for granted and goes unnoticed. For example, in Disney's *Tarzan*, the dapples of light on the characters' bodies were the result of a painstaking job performed by the effects department. Despite the long hours it took to accomplish, it goes almost unnoticed. But because of its very innocuousness, it succeeds in placing the characters more firmly in their environment, giving a greater illusion of a lived-in space. It bridges the gap between character and layout, and homogenises the final image. And dramatically, in a plot that concerns itself with ideas of family and home, it gives a more intense sense of the encompassing womb-like space of the jungle, which curves its leaves and branches around the bodies in its midst.

'For an effects-driven narrative, which demonstrates the sometimes volatile tensions between effects and character animation, there are few sequences better suited than "The Sorcerer's Apprentice" from *Fantasia* (1940). In his essay "The Animation of Sound", Philip Brophy examines the use of sound synchronisation in Disney and Warner Bros. animations, and pays particular attention to sequences from Disney's *Fantasia*.[2]

'He notes how fluid substances represent the dynamic flow of the music. By extension, it is possible to consider the water effect in "The Sorcerer's Apprentice" as moving towards actually representing the ethereal and abstract form of the music it strives to signify. The overproduction of water in the narrative, working both literally and metaphorically as a special effects layer, threatens to overcome its character animation counterpart. It thereby illustrates the tensions between character and effects as suggested by Klein earlier. In this sequence, the employment of warped glass and the mix of dry brush with traditional cel painting, the evocative use of shadow and the excellent realisation of water's substance, all help to display the multifaceted discipline of an effects artist.

'Even though there may be some aesthetic tensions between effects and character artwork, to achieve the complex spectacle of an animated feature film, close coordination between departments is absolutely necessary. Since the effects level is usually the final level of drawing to be produced on any given scene, the effects artist must pay close attention to the other levels on the X-sheet and liaise with other departments whenever necessary. Placing the scene

NOTE

2. P. Brophy, 'The Animation of Sound', in A. Cholodenko (ed.), *The Illusion of Life* (Sydney: Power Publications, 1991).

in the context of its sequence is also important to preserve continuity in design and action. Developing a strong design sense and a good vocabulary of abstract shapes is also important. Although the effects artist is usually supplied with a design workbook – which is similar to a character animator's model sheet – especially on such design-heavy productions like *Hercules* (Disney, 1997) and *Mulan* (Disney, 1998), they are still required to invent new forms in the process of keying the animation, while also maintaining the overall aesthetic style of the film.

'Observation of physical phenomena is the most important activity for an effects artist. To a certain degree, this brings us back to the concept of effects practice as "the zen of animation", where the artist is immersed in contemplation of the natural world. Therefore, observation of physical phenomena is of utmost importance if an effective sense of timing is to be developed. This is particularly important if the production is engaged in a hyper-realist aesthetic.'

15.2
Stills from Orange Telecommunications' advertisements – Studio AKA (Tim Robertson and Steve Little)
Studio AKA embraces a range of visual effects and stunning graphic design in its commercial output, demonstrating that the advertisement can also function as an experimental film.

Critical Evaluation

Throughout the process of creating any animated film there needs to be a degree of objectivity in monitoring progress and evaluating each aspect of the work as it unfolds.

Critical evaluation may be achieved in a number of ways at both a 'pragmatic' and 'artistic' level. For example, it remains crucial to constantly check budget and resources as the film is being executed. Similarly, all the technical aspects – that may include equipment checking through to file saving – must be addressed as the core facilitation aspects of the project.

Crucially, the developmental creative elements of the project need constant assessment and attention. The creation of an animated film in many senses relies on its pre-production process to ensure the success of the project. It is no accident that PIXAR takes so long on the script stage of its films before embarking on the animation itself. Preparation is vital and should be informed by a critically engaged set of choices about design and execution. Facilitating the inciting idea, the key narrative elements, and the thematic and conceptual premises of the work are constant preoccupations throughout the creative process. While technical errors sometimes have some points of redress, it is very hard to recover a piece of work that is narratively, aesthetically or conceptually flawed. Care and attention in the pre-production phase should ensure intended and successful outcomes.

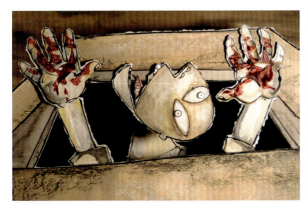

16.1

**Preparatory work and stills from *God on Our Side* –
Michal Pfeffer and Uri Kranot**

God on Our Side is a superb example of the way in which a personal
film can engage with a research process thematically, artistically
and technically, and succeed as emotionally profound and politically
invested work. The film stands up to extensive critical evaluation
by its makers, its viewers and those who seek to learn from the
practices of others.

AUTHOR TIP

Evaluation guidelines

Here are some key questions to pose when looking back on a project and some sample answers from an imaginary film, which might be critically helpful in improving practice when embarking on a new project.

What aspects of the process – artistically or technically – prompted the greatest degree of satisfaction and why?

The designs for the soldiers were historically accurate and came out of research at a military museum. The uniforms were adjusted to make sure that there were not too many elements that would be difficult to animate. Using Photoshop proved really helpful at that stage.

What aspects of the process – artistically or technically – posed problems or difficulties, and how were they resolved?

The main issue was time management. Everything took longer than expected and that meant corners had to be cut. Problems were resolved by improvising ways in which action could be suggested without actually being seen, or through minimal imagery. Also, a sequence was mislaid and took an age to recover. This caused tensions between the collaborators that had to be resolved. The answer was having clearer roles and responsibilities, and better organisation. Also, the 3D bits in Maya were a bit beyond our expertise. These were mostly replaced by 2D sequences.

As a consequence of thinking about these former questions, what can be identified as the core strengths and weaknesses of the approach to, and execution of, the project?

The strengths were in the quality and detail of the script, which enabled the pre-production process to go relatively smoothly. There was a realisation, too, that the work should be mainly in 2D as we could draw well but were less able using the 3D software. The weaknesses were in the ways in which disorganisation and not using time effectively disrupted the team.

Having identified the strengths and weaknesses of the process, how does this translate into an evaluation of core skills and knowledge – what are the key skills that have been gained and what are the main things that have been learned?

Key skills would be the technical quality of the script designs and full-drawn 2D animation, including persuasive lip-synch. The project clearly shows the capacity to 'animate'. The main thing learned would be the necessity to make sure that the script is completely right before starting.

In retrospect, what are the key strengths and weaknesses of the final outcome of the project? What aspects have been most successful, and why? If it were possible to change something, what should be changed and why?

The opening of the film was successful because it was achieved purely visually and used the soundtrack to evoke concern for the main character. The battle scene was also effective because instead of making it look epic through showing thousands of soldiers ready to fight, it showed the battle from within, with close-ups of injured bodies and falling horses. The 'love interest' aspect of the narrative should be changed – it slows down the story and doesn't add much in relation to the main character.

What set of 'recommendations' or 'conclusions' can be drawn from evaluating the project, which will be useful on another occasion?

The key recommendations would be to have a better planned schedule and to stick to it. To be more clear about roles and responsibilities. To make sure that the right technique is chosen and there is competence in using the equipment and software. Finally, to look at the script again – it seemed just right – but the problem about the 'love interest' was in there all along, with fairly pointless scenes.

Comment: This response is honest and enabling. It stresses the importance and usefulness of research; the necessity to keep redrafting the script, constantly asking hard questions of its narrative strength and its suitability for animation; the need to be clear and honest about technical competences and the techniques required for the project; the significance of project management and effective collaboration at all levels; and, finally, the fundamental belief in the idea and what can be achieved.

Portfolio

One of the key aspects of becoming a professional animator and working in the creative industries in general is the ability to present a portfolio to a potential employer. This is usually a CV (or résumé), a show reel and the materials that may be presented for interview. In the contemporary era, there is also the possibility of showcasing work on personal websites and in a range of formats for cross-platform presentation.

If applying for a specific position, it is important to find out the exact requirements of the role, and, most importantly, what is required by the company at the point of application. It is also important to know what the company does and its expectations of the people who work for it. This can often be obtained on company websites or in informal phone or email exchanges with recruitment personnel at the company.

Chris Bowden, Senior Producer at Cosgrove Hall Films, manages the recruitment of new animators and other personnel for Cosgrove Hall's productions. Bowden emphasises three aspects of a great portfolio:

- the pertinence of the show reel;
- the relevance of the CV;
- the discipline of the work itself.

Bowden: 'A CV and a show reel should be indicators of seriousness and commitment to the serious demands of the art and craft of animation. Only by demonstrating a professional investment in the form will the possibility of a professional opportunity become available.

'When attending an interview, it is important to be articulate about any work previously undertaken, and to show pertinent examples of pre-production work and production work that has been realised. In answering questions it is useful to signal knowledge of the company's work; the pertinence of, and evidence for, relevant skills; and, most importantly, a level of critical and creative understanding that shows autonomy, independence and initiative, while being committed to a collaborative and industrious ethos. As in any job, a good sense of humour is a standard requirement.'

EXPERT ADVICE

Chris Bowden's tips for job applications:

- The thing we look for most in an animation show reel, is (not surprisingly) an ability to animate. We look for examples of animation where there has been some thought and sensitivity applied to the movement.
- Most companies are inundated with reels, so make a concise collection of your best shots or sequences at the beginning. Add full-length films after. While pop video editing is certainly clever and flashy, it rarely gives the viewer a chance to actually see the animation clearly. Remember what you're trying to achieve.
- Try to keep your CV to a page in length, two at most. Avoid using smaller type just to fit more on; it makes the reader's eyes hurt.
- It may sound obvious, but at an interview or on work experience, be enthusiastic! It's a quality that can't be trained into an individual and counts a lot. Animation is a painstaking process and invariably involves a lot of hours spent standing up under hot lights. You have to want to do it more than (almost) anything.
- Be prepared to work as part of a team. Broadly speaking, television series animation is a collaborative effort. Your shots will be most effective when they enhance the telling of the story and work with all the other shots from all the other animators. Every shot can't be a splashy show reel number.
- Television series animation will provide a well of experience for animators, but requires a certain discipline. Typical series demand 10–15 seconds a day on average, so be prepared that you cannot always spend the amount of time you'd like to on a shot.
- Try to find the creative challenge in what you're doing: think, 'How can I make my shot great in the time I have?' rather than sweeping your hand across your brow and screaming, 'How can I perform under these conditions?'!

Show Reel

—

The standard requirements for a show reel are simple and straightforward:

- Reels should be online or on DVD.
- Include a detailed credit list/reel breakdown explaining what you did on each shot (including techniques) and what software (if applicable) was used to achieve the effects.
- The length of your reel should be no longer than five minutes and consist of work that you're most proud of, starting with your best, most recent work.
- Music isn't necessary.

This takes into account format, supporting technical information, the 'best at the front' rule (it is likely only two minutes, at most, will be watched of any reel), and the subtle guidance that a hip-hop groove or high-end guitar riff in support of a rapid edit may not best show work to the most impressive advantage.

A number of colleges and universities, particularly in regard to the presentation of CGI skills, recommend a two-minute show reel demonstrating the process of construction (rigging, rendering etc.), before the revelation of the final character/environment in a short narrative situation. Also, in such a sequence – for any animation discipline – showing lip-synch (using pertinent vocal delivery and sound mixing, not merely an engaging piece of music) and a particular movement, which demonstrates a knowledge of the core skills of animating, are also helpful in showing particular and necessary abilities.

The show reel must ultimately impress: first, by demonstrating core skills executed to a high level of achievement, and second, by showing individual flare and talent in choices and presentation.

CV/Résumé

—

It is often the case that individuals create a CV for themselves and send it to any potential employer or for any available post, unrevised. In a highly competitive field, CVs need to be made relevant to each application and be revised if necessary. The 'relevance' of a CV to a particular post or role is crucial because it is likely that such a post will have highly specific tasks and required outcomes.

CVs, of course, also have to evolve and become 'working' documents because different levels of achievement and ability will necessarily have to be presented in different ways as a career unfolds. A student, for example, will have to present what they have achieved as a student in relation to the course undertaken, any work experience and some measure of the standard and achievement in what has been done. A slightly more experienced professional might have gained other skills and done more work, so needs to present that accordingly. An even more experienced person may have a list of credits, but it is crucial that a CV does not merely turn into a list and remains an accurate but appealing and impressive document about a specific individual – you.

The presentation of a CV is very important, but there is a fine line between over-elaborating the design and creating an engaging, easy-to-read document. The information in a CV is the most important aspect of it, but clearly that can be ordered and presented in a number of different ways. This is closely related to the need to revise a CV to make it relevant to a particular employer, if necessary. Indeed, many employers now provide a CV cover sheet indicating the core information required, and this may make a personal CV almost redundant. In such an instance, a CV must offer more detail and place greater emphasis on personality, skills and achievements.

WHAT'S A SHOWREEL AND WHY DO I NEED ONE TO BECOME AN ANIMATOR?

A showreel is a compilation of the best bits of your animation and is a vital asset for any aspiring animator – it's a way for you to show off your skills and show potential employers why they need you in their organisation! In the words of one of Aardman's veteran animators:

> "Your showreel is your one chance to shine without necessarily being present. It needs to demonstrate, in a couple of minutes, the genius of years of hard work. It's not just a compilation: it's the unique you and your life ambitions condensed into a few minutes. It's also the ticket to your future."

When compiling a showreel, remember that it will probably be viewed alongside those of other animators. Be creative and original, put your best work first and make sure your reel stands out. Don't forget when compiling your showreel that film companies will be looking for examples of your animation skills as well, so include a segment that demonstrates walk cycles or stretch and squash moments.

Finally, before submitting your work, remember that all animation companies will have their own submission policy. This must be read in full before you send your showreel to them.

CAN I SEND AARDMAN MY SHOWREEL OR PORTFOLIO?

Yes, absolutely. In fact, if you're applying for a creative role of some sort at Aardman, we need to see some examples of work – usually in the format of a showreel or artwork – to help us appraise your talents. Please note that we can't accept showreels or portfolios on email so please send us your application and supporting materials to us in the post at the following address:

> Human Resources, Aardman Animations, Gas Ferry Road, Bristol BS1 6UN

Unfortunately we are unable to return showreels, portfolios or other materials so please do not send originals, always send copies of work. When preparing your showreel please consider the following:

— A showreel should ideally be between 3–6 mins in length.

— Please do not send links to a website or attachments.

— Always present your best work first. A running order is also advisable, and if you didn't animate all the work include a description of your contribution on the showreel.

— If you have experience in more than one area then include relevant examples.

— Remember to clearly mark your name and contact details on everything!

— Be specific about what position you want to apply for – don't forget to include a CV coversheet and a full CV.

Due to the high volume of showreels we receive, it may take up to 12 weeks for the reviewing process to be complete. A delay in response doesn't mean a lack of interest and if we think there's a vacancy that matches your skill set, we'll be in touch!

17.1

Guidelines for show reels

Aardman Animation's show reel requirements are very similar to those listed in the text, but have additional and very helpful detail. More information can be found at www.aardman.com/faq/

Improve your CV/résumé

—

Blue Sky Resumes addresses these issues, and advises on the presentational aspects of CVs, predominantly in the American marketplace, and across disciplines and institutions. The following 'before' and 'after' comparison shows how material can be better presented to enhance the credentials of any one individual.

Though this is only one example, notice the difference between presenting a 'bare bones' CV with phone contact, listed career history and basic education, and presenting a statement with an understated design motif, full contact details, a personal summary with an endorsement from a senior figure, a focus on professional highlights before a more detailed career history informed by its key roles and achievements, additional but relevant work, like teaching and public speaking, and education and core technical skills. Self-evidently, this will vary from person to person and it may be that 'education' and 'technical' skills come much higher in the document, but more than anything else the CV offers a more comprehensive and appealing statement about the person. With care and thought, something similarly impressive can be constructed at whatever stage of a career you may be at. Many people 'naturalise' the things they do and don't think of them as 'skills' and 'achievements'. This is particularly important in the early stages of a career when there will inevitably be less experience and external achievement. It is vital, therefore, to think through the production process undertaken in any educational context to state if there has been strength in preparation and organisation, script development, technical skills, collaboration and teamwork, research etc. The role of work experience, other courses, festivals and events attended, and extra-curricular activities may also be very significant indicators of additional skills, knowledge and investment in an area.

A CV is a statement about you. Make it informative and attractive, but most importantly, make it relevant to the employment sought.

Mona Vinar
555.555.5555 home
555.555.5555 cell

Career History:

2008 – Present   **Director**, DVD
                   Highlights: *A Lion's Story*
                   ForKids Animations, San Francisco, CA

2007 – 2008   **Director**, feature film
                   Highlights: *The Moose and the Bluebird*
                   ForKids Animations, San Francisco, CA

2005 – 2007   **Animation Director**, Direct-to-Home Video/DVDs
                   Highlights: *The Spider Makes a Friend*
                   Six Cats and a Mouse
                   ForKids Animations, San Francisco, CA

2003 – 2005   **Senior Animator**, Various
                   Highlights: *The Boy Who Loved Christmas*
                   ForKids Animations

2004 – Present   Instructor, Animation Department
                   New York University

2000 – 2003   **3D Artist/Animator**, Various TV Productions
                   Highlights: *Two Small Pigs*
                   Pixen, Inc.

1998 – 2003   **Contract Artist/Proprietor**
                   Movin' Graphic Design

Studies:

BA, Graphic Design, NYU
MA, Computer Graphics and Animation, UCLA

17.2a

Before and After: A dummy CV demonstrating the value of presentation – Blue Sky Resumes

Though considerable emphasis is placed on the show reel in a practice context, an impressive CV page can be a strong indicator of the person, the profile and the appropriateness of a candidate to a role. This example offers the 'bare bones'.

MONA VINAR

3 Bentley Place
New York, NY 55555
H: 555.555.5555
C: 555.555.5555
E-Mail: monavinar@jupiter.com

AWARD-WINNING ANIMATION DIRECTOR
Video – Film – Television

Senior Director whose work has been widely recognized and honored. Proven track record of leading studio teams to produce innovative animation in a variety of media. Combines a visionary creative philosophy with outstanding technical skills, strong leadership abilities and a true passion for animation excellence.

"Mona is a rare find because she has strong technical knowledge combined with exceptional people skills. This allows her to keep everyone upbeat during a project while still getting excellent results."

John Doe, Former Production Executive, Dreamworks and ForKids

PROFESSIONAL HIGHLIGHTS

- Directed full length animated feature which won the 2009 Silver Jewel award for Best Children's Film. Variety Magazine said *"the computer animation is truly dazzling."*
- Conceived, wrote and directed animated short film which was honored at the LA Children's Film Festival and the New York Animation Film Festival.
- Director of Animation for home video which was the recipient of 6 awards including the New York Film Board Award of Excellence and selection as 2010 International Animation Festival Winner.

PROFESSIONAL HISTORY

ForKids Animations   **2003-2012**

- o Animation Director (2007 – Present)
- o Animation Manager (2005 – 2007)
- o Senior Animator (2003 – 2005)

Advanced rapidly to the position of Animator Director with responsibility for creative design direction including story and script, talent casting, visual concept, character development and camera layout.

- Directed *The Moose and the Bluebird*, which remained on Billboard's top ten movie list for 7 weeks and garnered critical acclaim from Variety, Hollywood Reporter, LA Times and Animation magazine.
- Animation Director for *The Spider Makes a Friend*, winner of 6 awards including Animator's World Award of Excellence and 2007 Silver Telly award for exceptional children's entertainment.
- Animation Supervisor for 2003 television special *The Boy Who Loved Christmas* which has aired annually for the last nine years.

17.2b

A good deal of thought and attention should go into the preparation and presentation. Notice the difference between this and the previous example.

Collaboration

Due to current funding strategies most contemporary animation production involves collaboration. There are often tax incentives for international projects, or other economic drivers such as comparative wages that may be paid to animators inside and outside Europe or the USA. This results in feature films and series that are designed in one country and realised in several others through partnerships between the originators of the idea, animation companies, production houses, merchandisers and distributors.

Animation series are often created with the intention to broadcast them in many languages and therefore there can be a 'dumbing down' of strong cultural identities in order for these films to be regarded as commercially viable in the international media market. This can affect any aspect of the production from background design (homogenised environments rather than localised landscapes), to actual behaviour of characters (more likely to be seen eating burgers than noodles or fish and chips).

But new markets for animated series, films and commercials are developing across the world. Recent research into Middle Eastern animation broadcasting content suggests that currently it does not include any distinctive children's animation series containing aspects of language, culture and heritage that Arab parents and children may identify with. The majority of children's programmes aired on Arab networks are supplied by entertainment providers from the West

and the Far East, which are unlikely to satisfy the growing demand for animation productions made with cultural sensitivity, as media influence in the Muslim world grows.

Faisal and Friends (see Character Development on pp. 54–55) is a series in development that is targeted at this new audience and is being created through cross-cultural collaboration between Aladdin Media Limited (London), Ugly Studios UK and Imprint Studios in Egypt.

Characters and environmental designs have been developed by animators at Ugly in close collaboration with Aladdin, every step in the process being vetted for Muslim sensibilities. Islamic designs are incorporated into the whole fabric of the production, from the plants in the animated world to textures on the characters' skin and clothing.

18.1

Sketches and still from *Faisal and Friends*

The series follows the adventures of Faisal, a young frog and his friends, grasshopper Saleem, butterfly Laila, snail Professor Aamir and fish Mrs Jamila, who all live in or next to a pond. The set of characters represents family figures and they have different skin colours, reflecting the diversity of Islamic origin. The scripts promote ideas about responsible world citizenship and are not exclusive to a Muslim audience.

As with most CGI animation, the original visuals are all hand drawn and in this case are emailed to Imprint Studios for 3D realisation. A strong dialogue and mutual respect has developed between the animators in both countries, daily image swaps and critiques helping to ensure a common vision of the project.

Cathal Gaffney of Brown Bag Films, Dublin, has been engaged with international collaboration, animating commercials for the Middle Eastern market since 1997.

Gaffney: 'We have a good system of approval that is done over the Internet either by email or by downloading larger files from our FTP site. We are in the process of installing a Telestream system that will allow us to send completed files directly to the broadcasters.'

In 2004, Brown Bag won the prestigious Phoenix award for work on a series of commercials for Pampa Juice featuring Jean Luc. This involved a live-action shoot of Jean Luc against a green screen background in Beirut. Then they took the footage back to Ireland and produced a locked-off edit from which they created a series of 3D animated characters and 3D background elements.

Brown Bag Films also rebranded Saudi Arabian state television, which involved creating over 80 motion graphic identities.

Gaffney: 'When doing business with the Middle East it is normal to haggle over quotes for any job and you must not be surprised by passionate positive and negative reactions to the work in progress. Creative directors in the Middle East have a great knowledge of visual language, so once the animation is underway, there is no discernable difference between working for a client there than anywhere else. Details such as the phonetic breakdown of Arabic to get lip-synch working correctly can be difficult but most people we deal with speak perfect English so it's not too much of a problem.'

Faisal and Friends is based on characters created by Aladdin Media, but Ugly Studios redesigned them with the audience in mind, then Imprint Studios took the drawings into CGI. This is not design by committee; each part of the process is clearly owned, although consultation continues throughout. All scripts and designs are approved by Aladdin Media before the next stage is undertaken, ensuring that the right tone and message is maintained.

18.2

**Stills from Pampa Juice commercials –
Brown Bag Films**

International collaboration on advertisements
is common, but requires a particular sensitivity
to 'local' audiences in relation to humour,
recognisable characters and events, and the nature
of the product.

18.3

Stills from Saudi Arabian state television news programme identities – Brown Bag Films

Brown Bag Films create an 'international' identity to the introductory idents by using iconography common to station
branding and news coverage elsewhere, while privileging the key identifying imagery of the station and its delivery.

Working as an Independent

'Employability' in the animation and creative industries can be understood in a number of ways.

The 'portfolio' discussed earlier is largely constructed with studio/independent companies in mind, and is concerned with applying for particular posts or work experience opportunities. Employment can be gained in other ways, but requires a different approach if it is to be achieved either through forming an independent company, or seeking grants or other kinds of funding to make an independent film, both of which may be intrinsically related.

Second Home Studios

—

Second Home Studios was set up in response to a series of commissions for theatre projection design. Director Chris Randall: 'We got to the point where we needed to be a limited company for insurance reasons. At the time it was a bit of a necessity – the name was a joke because we never went home! – and it just grew from there, really.'

Their initial start in theatre projection was their staple work for a while when they first started, but they soon began to veer more towards pure animation, with an emphasis on stop-motion. The company has been going since 2004 and has been in its current premises in Digbeth, Birmingham since 2006. It is set over two floors and took four months to gut and rebuild the interior to make it studio-worthy. 'We've kept the space and kit as versatile as possible, where we can easily think on our feet, but our biggest asset as a company is the people we work with like Ian [Whittle], Adam [Watts] and Tilley [Bancroft].

'We had help from Creative Launchpad [at the Custard Factory, Birmingham] in the form of a small grant, but we also had money from previous jobs and so we could get started. We got a DigiShorts commission [short film commission from the Film Council UK] shortly after starting the company, so *The Animal Book* [2007] was a way to show what we could do.

'Since then the portfolio's grown in ways we couldn't imagine and we've done some pretty ambitious things like the Pilsner [commercial, see pp. 30–35] commission. Where possible we like to be involved in the writing and development stage as much as possible. A good example of this is *The Mechanical Musical Marvel*. The script went through 36 iterations before we drew a single cell, but it paid off as it ended up on BAFTA's radar in their Children's Animation category, and it continues to screen around the world.'

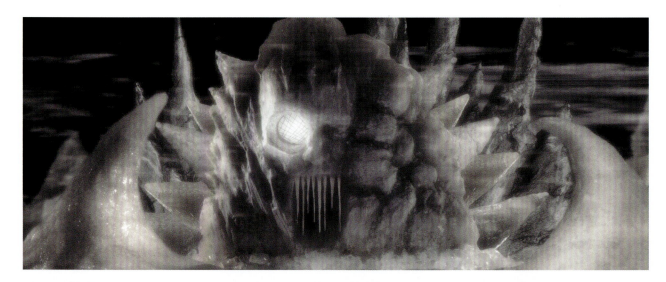

19.1

Theatre projection designs for *The Lion, the Witch and the Wardrobe* by Second Home Studios.

19.2
Sequence for *Sky at Night* (BBC, 2011). The intro sequence for *Sky at Night* was shot in silhouette.
The 'binoculars' used in the sequence were knocked up in the workshop from remnants in the recycling bin.

Second Home is continuing to develop its own intellectual property, working on series concepts, ideas for the digital domain as well as a new short film. Chris is represented by Picasso Pictures for directing commercial work.

Chris's advice to people setting up their own studio is to try and get regular contract work, however modest. He says that during start-up everyone involved needs to work equally hard at making the studio a success: 'It does help if everyone's work ethic is the same, and we've been lucky, but it can cause friction and problems if people's loyalty is divided. Your team *is* the company, effectively.' Chris suggests that getting a mentor is wise, to help trouble-shoot problems and give guidance. 'Expect things to get hard, expect the ride to be bumpy.' 'If there's things you don't know, either get someone who does know how to do it or give yourself a chance to learn.' He loves being involved in all aspects of studio work, but working through a performance with other animators is easily his favourite part. 'There is a reason you do the long hours, when you hit play and it all comes to life.'

The Pitfalls

—

Brown Bag's Cathal Gaffney had a different and in some senses more problematic experience.

Gaffney: 'At that time there was another incubation scheme called ICE (Irish Creative Enterprise), which helped start up small businesses. I didn't want to start a business really. All I wanted to do was to make my own little art films. I had made another short film and that won first prize at the Galway Film Fleah – it was called *Rush* and was a rendered fine art animation piece, and I did another called *Expressive Dimensions*. I was working on an idea about an old woman from the West of Ireland called Peig Sayers, who did nothing with her life except write a book about her hardship and misery, and it was inflicted on students for decades in Ireland, and everybody hated it, and people would not speak a word of Irish after studying it, all their school lives. I, and the guys I was working with, wanted to take the living piss out of Peig, and absolutely get our own back for all the hassle she had inflicted on us! So we approached RTE and they said, go ahead and make the series.

'We didn't have a clue about budgets and contracts, and I did not know about VAT numbers, and we did not know what we were doing. This TV series was worth 50 grand; we'd go down to the bank and take out £1500, and give it out, without receipts or invoices, or anything. We were the best example of how not to do a business. It was sink or swim, but we made the series in 1994 and it was very popular and is still remembered today. The nation was talking about it. We thought we were going to be media moguls and be loaded. But nothing happened. That was the end of it. Later, we went to the bank with another business plan, and they said "No". Our parents became our guarantors on a loan, though, and we moved to Gardner Place. We had an electric typewriter, a photocopier, two months' rent, and a whole lot of drawing desks!

'This was in 1995 and for about two years we did subcontracted service animation for other studios – King Rollo, Honeycomb – episodes *of Wolves, Witches and Giants* and the like, so we all did drawing animation on it. We learned a lot about production procedures. We moved again and got a computer! We wanted to develop our own ideas again. We did inserts for a TV programme called *Barstool* and sold it to BBC Choice and the Paramount Comedy Channel. Very slowly we were building things up organically. We never got any big investors. We did another TV series called *Taxi* about Dublin taxi drivers and that was very popular too. At that stage, we set up a company called Brown Bag Development, so we could keep all the intellectual property rights separate from all the bread-and-butter leases and loans, staffing costs etc. of the production company.

'All the time it was not easy. We got a few ads and some CD-ROM work, and work for other companies, but we wanted to develop our own ideas. We developed a 13-part, half-hour animation series in children's cartoon style, which bombed. More than anything, the ultimate aim was still to pay yourself, and your staff, so we had to get critical mass to do that, and only after that was it about the kind of work you want to do. You subsidise personal work through commercial business. For a while you have to recognise that you have more in common with the local shopkeeper than the artist. It has to be about commerciality and profit first.'

AUTHOR TIP

Points to consider in forming an independent company

- Seek advice from a number of sources about setting up a business. Consult with established small businesses, banks, business support organisations and anyone who might offer relevant professional acumen.

- Look to Business Enterprise and Incubation schemes as possible ways of establishing a company. Equally, seek out an established company to mentor the development of a new enterprise.

- Try to associate your company with a network of geographically or professionally close businesses and organisations. Sometimes being in a 'business park' can be helpful in sharing information, resource and custom.

- Get as much information and support as possible from regional arts and media organisations, and constantly look for funding opportunities.

- Create the best show reel possible to signal the ethos, potential and talent of the company. Constantly update the reel as work is completed.

- Seek out small-scale, low-level, cost-effective work in the first instance to build the show reel and portfolio of the company. Potential clients need evidence of quality and achievement related to economic sense. Trailers, advertisements, interstitials, CD-ROM inserts etc. are required in a number of broadcast and exhibition outlets. Make enquiries in a number of contexts to seek out possible contracts for comparatively small-scale work.

- Enter competitions, festivals, exhibitions etc. and use any context to promote the identity, quality and distinctiveness of the company's work.

- Seek out subcontracted work with more established companies.

- Try and establish a 'core idea' for an investment project, which may be pitched to larger organisations and broadcast outlets. This may be a more 'personal' project or one that seeks to compete in the established professional arena, but, hopefully, it will be a 'breakthrough' project that succeeds in gaining the company more work and other creative opportunities.

- Keep the artistic, technical and commercial principles of the company under constant review in order to make strategic and operational decisions to develop the organisation.

- Establish a supportive network of parents, friends and professional colleagues to help you endure difficult times or unsuccessful periods.

- Try to sustain confidence, the courage of conviction, enthusiasm and the commitment to hard work, sometimes with little reward, as the company grows.

- Remember that all success is hard earned, should be enjoyed and used to sustain 'a career' – this is not a hobby anymore!

Postgraduate Opportunties

In what is now a hugely competitive area of work, success at undergraduate level or other training initiatives may not be sufficient. If, having read the demands of a portfolio or CV, or the requirements in setting up an independent company, it is clear that more training or experience may be required, then postgraduate courses may be beneficial.

Why Continue Your Study?
—

If you embark on a degree it is likely that the first year will be an uphill climb, where learning the basics necessitates a lot of diagnostic and advisory support. The second year tends to be much more consolidatory and many students properly engage with the tasks and assessments with much more acumen and insight for the first time. Only in the third year – or fourth year on some deliveries – does work feel potentially autonomous and independent. This can be the springboard for seeking work immediately, but for many it is a time to take stock and sustain achievement in a postgraduate context. Many of the young animators in this book have undertaken a postgraduate course because it has been an opportunity for them to fully understand what stage they are at in their development and to make work that more fully represents their ability, outlook and potential. It is often such work that can be confidently sent to festivals, potential employers, or funding councils to enhance the possibility of more opportunities.

20.1

Still from *I Married a Strange Person* – Bill Plympton

Many postgraduate courses have a number of visiting professionals who help and advise on working practices and careers in animation. Independent Bill Plympton, for example, has conducted many workshops and offered pertinent advice about entering the sector.

20.2

Production shots from the making of *God on Our Side* – Michal Pfeffer and Uri Kranot

The Netherlands Institute of Animated Film, where Pfeffer and Kranot made their film, is a post-academic workshop that offers young artists and film-makers the opportunity to work on animation and research projects for a two-year period in their own studio, with a budget, grant aid, and professional help and support.

Choosing a Course

—

The choice of a postgraduate course is important and requires a lot of research – information is freely available on the Web, but requesting prospectuses and making visits to the places of study is crucial. Each course will have its own ethos and agenda. Take, for example, the following cases:

Royal College of Art – 'The Animation programme is a world leader in practice and research, with a commitment to broadening the understanding of our complex discipline. We offer a unique learning and teaching environment, developing the creativity and skills required in an age of rapid cultural and technological change to enable students to contribute to this expanding and maturing field of moving image.

'Through innovative, practical research and an understanding of different contexts, traditions and histories, students learn through a potent combination of workshops, lectures, tutorials and, most importantly, through their own practice.'

Bournemouth University National Centre for Computer Animation – 'This animation course has been designed to introduce students to all aspects of computer animation: Modelling, Texturing, Rigging, Lighting, Dynamics, Compositing and Scripting.

'The course aims to enable students to become creative practitioners in computer animation with a good understanding of the inter-relation of aesthetic, perceptual ad technical factors involved in the development of computer animation productions.'

La Poudriere, Ecole du Film d'Animation – 'Wholly dedicated to creation, resolutely professional, a great place on the artistic side. A place where students can take classes, make films and meet key industry professionals. Two principal aims: to train and nurture creative talent to develop the art of animation; to contribute to the creative evolution of a quality cinema.'

CalArts MFA Experimental Animation – 'Fine art principles and practices are the essential forces guiding the mission of the Program in Experimental Animation – a course of study designed for independent and adventurous artists who are interested in personal expression and who regard animation as an ever-evolving art form. This program offers a framework in which students explore, develop and refine intellectually demanding, aesthetically progressive concepts and professional practices in their personal cinematic art making. The Program in Experimental Animation enjoys a long-standing international reputation for excellence in innovative animation production. Its faculty, students and alumni have consistently won top awards at film festivals in the United States, Europe and Asia, and are widely credited with helping to define the art of animation as we know it today.'

These are not merely statements about the courses; they are statements of principle about approaches to animation as an art, a craft, a technique, a means of expression, a mode of employment and an attitude to life. Careful attention is required to choose the right course for an individual's personal development and needs. Make contact with the key personnel on courses and visit institutions before and after application. Make choices on fully informed grounds and in relation to career aspirations.

Making an Independent Film

In 1967, UBU Films in Australia created a manifesto that insisted upon the idea that an independent abstract film could be made under any circumstances. It was designed to reject the 'studio' ethos and to encourage the disempowered creative person or experimental artist to make their work and not be inhibited by financial or contextual constraints. While the manifesto is of its 'countercultural' time, the ideas still apply and have some currency, nearly 50 years later (see Manifesto opposite).

A less avant-garde, radical perspective is offered by independent animator Bill Plympton, who, by a range of strategies – making shorts as parts of features or as vehicles by which to fund longer work, working on the Web etc. – seeks to create independent work in a contemporary commercial context.

Plympton: 'The first rule is to keep the film short – about two or three minutes – because it is much easier for a festival or for a TV station to programme it and for a compilation programmer to include it. My films are about five minutes, although I have done an eight/nine-minute short.

'The second rule is to make the film cheaply. The audience doesn't really care that much if it is loaded with special effects or loaded with orchestral music or fancy digital imagery – they want to see the characters; they want to see a simple story told by engaging characters. I tried to keep the cost down to $1000–$2000 a minute. If you can keep your costs down to a low level then it is much easier getting your money back.

'The third rule is the most important part for me: to make it funny. I don't make the rules; I don't dictate what the make-up of the audience anywhere is, but in general the audience likes to laugh and for some reason expects to laugh at animation. Now, there are a lot of film-makers who make beautiful, sensitive films, or political films, or more artistic films – like Michael Dudok de Wit, for example, who makes serious films and is very successful – but, in general, that's a rarity and funny animation finds an audience quicker. That's great for me, because I grew up trying to draw funny cartoons and I like hearing people laugh. I like telling jokes and for me that is easy and luckily that's the main market. Visual humour can be universal – whether it is China, South America, Australia, or England, a visual joke plays almost exactly the same in every screening. I could be in a theatre in China or England and the laugh will come at the same time and with the same volume.'

21.1

**Production sketch and still from
God on Our Side – Michal Pfeffer
and Uri Kranot**

Pfeffer and Kranot drew upon
Picasso's *Guernica* thematically
and aesthetically in their design
work, which readily contextualised
the artistic and political agenda
of the piece. Allying form and
content is fundamental to the
emotional and philosophical
immediacy of the final film.

UBU Films Manifesto

01 – Let no one say anymore that they can't raise enough money to make a film – any film scrap can be turned into a hand-made film at no cost.

02 – Let photography be no longer essential to film-making – hand-made films are made without a camera.

03 – Let literary considerations of plot and story no longer be essential to film-making – hand-made films are abstract.

04 – Let no more consideration be given to direction and editing – hand-made films are created spontaneously.

05 – Let no media be denied to hand-made films – they can be scratched, scraped, drawn, inked, coloured, dyed, painted, pissed-on, black and white or coloured, bitten, chewed, filed, rasped, punctured, ripped, burned, blurred, bloodied, with any technique imaginable.

06 – Let written and performed music be rejected by makers of hand-made films – let hand-made music be created directly on to the film by any technique of scratching or drawing etc., imaginable.

07 – Let no orthodoxy of hand-made films be established – they may be projected alone, in groups, on top of each other, forward, backwards, slowly, quickly, in every possible way.

08 – Let no standard of hand-made films be created by critics – a film scratched inadvertently by a projector is equal to a film drawn explicitly by a genius.

09 – Let hand-made films not be projected in cinemas, but as environments, not to be absorbed intellectually, but by all senses.

10 – Most of all, let hand-made film-making be open to everyone, for hand-made films must be popular art.

21.2

Stills from *Westerkerk* – Holly Rumble

These images are from Holly Rumble's film *Westerkerk* and are rotoscoped from video, through tiny prints from the timeline, with crayon drawn over to emphasise selective aspects. These images were then re-filmed. The effect is one of enhancement, but the hand-drawn element gives an organic, analogue impression of what is otherwise a digital process. Holly Rumble undertook the MA in Animation and Sound Design at the Norwich School of Art and Design, UK.

Screening Opportunities

The most important part about being a creative person is not merely being creative in relation to the art form itself, but in the ways in which you can remain inventive and find an audience for the work and, in turn, stimulate more opportunities for the animator to gain work or present elsewhere.

Markets

In any walk of life, 'networking' is important. Getting to know people within the creative industries might lead to the possibility of work, exhibition or profile activity. Taking any opportunity and making the best of it, even if it is not the absolutely desired task or role, may facilitate other contacts and access to other projects and possibilities.

Independent animator Bill Plympton has had not merely to be 'an artist', but also an entrepreneur and an agent to promote his work. His short films ultimately funded longer films; his website has presented his work and sustained a profile; and his constant presence at festivals has enabled him to make contacts to facilitate more projects.

Plympton: 'After I did *Boomtown* I did get a reputation, as it was quite successful and I was approached at a party at a festival by a Russian émigré who said, "I want to give you $2000 to make your next film." At first I thought this was great, but I was lying in bed thinking that that would mean he would own the film and would get to dictate the content of that film. I suddenly realised that I had $2000 from my illustration work, and I thought if I don't believe in myself, why would I expect someone else to believe in me, so I invested my own money in *Your Face*, which cost $3000 and went on to make $30,000. I learned it is better to invest in your own film than have someone else invest in it, because whoever has the money has the power; that is the way it is in Hollywood and that is the way it is in life. I realised that I needed to have that film be a success, artistically and commercially, so I really pushed myself to make sure it would work and the audience would like it. A lot of "arty" film-makers are alien to that concept, but I always believe the audience should like the film. If you don't want them to like it, why show it and if you don't want to show it, why make it? If they like it, you get your money back.'

Plympton recognised that he needed to market and promote his own films and learned about negotiation and the specific sales of 'rights' to his work in different markets.

Plympton: 'Guys would come up to me and say we would like to offer you $1000 to show your film on our TV station and I would say, great, not knowing if I should ask for $5000 or $10,000 or whatever. I was just grateful for the money. So I hooked up with a distributor called Eteltoons, based in New York. They marketed short animated films throughout the world and had great success with *Allegro Non Tropo* and other Bruno Bozzetto and Guido Manuli films. I started getting regular quarterly cheques of $15,000 strictly from foreign rights, then I would get domestic rights from MTV, Tourneé of Animation, Spike and Mike shows, and individual TV stations, and I only knew about these people from the festival circuit because they would approach me. There are always new markets; someone says Cartoon Network is buying shorts now, or the BBC, or someone like Atom Films comes along, which distributes on the Internet, which gave me a flat fee, and helped me fund *Mutant Aliens* and they have the rights to sell in certain territories.'

Popular Animation Festivals Worldwide

Anima Mundi
São Paulo/Rio de Janeiro, Brazil

Animac
Lleida, Spain

Animerte Dager
Fredrikstad, Norway

Animex International Festival of Animation
University of Teesside, UK

Annecy: Centre International du Cinéma d'Animation
Annecy, France

Bradford Animation Festival, BAF
Bradford, UK

Brisbane International Animation Festival
Griffith University, Brisbane, Australia

Cartoons on the Bay: International Festival of TV Animation
Positiano, Italy

Cinema International Animation Festival
Chicago, USA

Encounters Festival
Bristol, UK

Fantoche International Animation Festival
Baden, Switzerland

Hiroshima International Animation Festival
Hiroshima, Japan

Holland Animation Festival, HAFF
Utrecht, The Netherlands

New York Animation Festival
New York, USA

Ottawa International Animation Festival
Ottawa, Canada

Spike and Mike's (Sick and Twisted) Festival of Animation
Touring, USA

Tricky Women – female animation festival
Vienna, Austria

Zagreb World Festival of Animated Films
Zagreb, Croatia

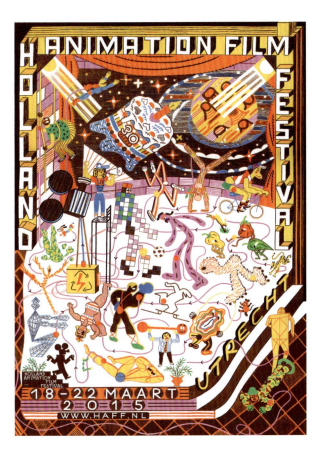

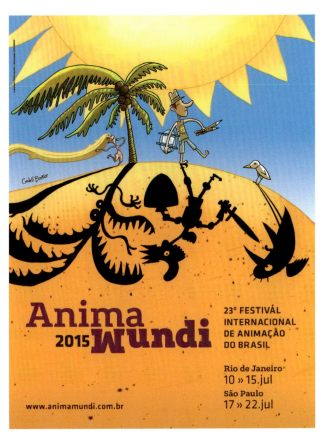

22.1
Poster for the Dutch HAFF Animation Film Festival, 2015.

22.2
Poster for the Brazilian Anima Mundi Animation Festival, 2015.

ONLY 2 DAYS MORE SCREENINGS!

22.3

A sketch of the Annecy student – Peter Parr

Festivals can be daunting prospects when you are used to working alone in a darkened room for the majority of the year, but here is where you find others like yourself, with a common purpose and goals like you.

Festivals

—

Animation festivals are in many senses the lifeblood of independent animation and the animation community. It is important to remember, though, that different festivals have different identities, some more specifically embracing individual 'auteurist' work, others prioritising commercial work in television and feature films. One need only note Annecy's 2015 festival in figures (see opposite/below), for example, to see the possible scale of international business negotiation and commercial outlets.

RAI Trade organises Cartoons on the Bay in Italy, also as a commercial platform, 'in order to sustain, in the spirit of public service that characterises RAI Italian TV and Radio Broadcasting Company, the effort of authors and producers worldwide [to] unite art to entertainment and to help buyers, TV distributors and executives, offering them a wide choice of successful and innovative products'. This then is more about economic issues and trade than it is about art and culture, although these issues can never be wholly marginalised in the consideration of appropriate, appealing and quality work in the field, whether it is for a popular audience or not.

The Fredrikstad Animerte Dager festival in Norway, however, has a much more educational, artistic and geographically sensitive stance to its operation. Practitioner, writer and historian Gunnar Strøm shares his thoughts.

Strøm: 'Fredrikstad could offer Animerte Dager a very attractive environment. That the city's own film and media industries are in rapid growth also gives the festival a valuable role to play beyond the festival weeks. The festival has now also been incorporated into the official arts programme for local schools. This local identity is an important and necessary building block as the festival looks towards its next ten years as the most important meeting point for animators from the Baltic and Nordic countries.'

One of the most anticipated festivals is the Ottawa International Animation Festival, whose artistic director, Chris Robinson, offers the following reasons why festivals are crucial to the budding professional animator.

Robinson: 'Despite the phenomenal growth of animation over the last two decades, animation festivals still remain one of the few places where independent animators can get their work shown to their peers and to a general audience.

'As such, this is an essential place for any aspiring animator to be. Not only will they see like-minded animation from all over the world, they will have an opportunity to meet their peers and share stories, ideas, develop friendships, partnerships etc. Festivals are an essential meeting place for animators – whether you want to go the indie or industry route.

'Awards are not so important in my view, but still, festivals are a place where your films are judged by your peers. It gives you some sense of where you stand, and heck, awards can help you get work/ funding in the future. But even without awards, it's so hard to get accepted into festival competitions that you should be pretty pleased just to get your film shown (even if it's a non-competitive showcase). As a comparison, consider the Oscars. You need money and friends to get your film entered for consideration. In the end, the Oscar for Short Animation has maybe 300 entries. That's a far cry from the 1500 or so entries that festivals like Annecy and Ottawa receive annually. Point? Animation festivals may not get you a trip to Hollywood or a TV appearance, but they are a significantly better gauge of short animation production than the Oscars.

'Festivals have this communal quality about them. It's a really special, unique opportunity (in this Internet age) to sit across a table from a person from another country and talk to them.

'If you want work, festivals like Annecy and Ottawa attract industry recruiters, buyers, producers. They're good places to network and you get to travel to places you might never venture (Hiroshima, Ottawa, Annecy, Zagreb, Utrecht, Stuttgart, Brazil).

'You spend a year working alone in a darkened room, probably wondering what the hell you're doing with your life making a "cartoon" that no one will see. Well, the animation community is relatively small and intimate, and there's a dysfunctional family quality to it. Attending festivals (with or without a film) is like going to a family reunion. It can be painful and tiring, but you're with your clan, your blood, your people. You belong to something, and isn't that what we all want at the end of the day? To connect with people with similar tastes and experiences?

'If you're still drooling to get an Oscar, here's the thing. If you win first prize in a category at Ottawa, Zagreb, Hiroshima or Annecy, you can skip the usual qualifications and have your film considered instantly for Oscar consideration. So there it is. What's not to like?'

Annecy 2015 festival in figures

8300 badge holders

More than **1000** exhibitors

Over **200** buyers including the main purchasers for children's programmes

83 countries represented

305 journalists

500 films screened

230 films in the official selection

An open-air giant screen

125,000 admissions during the week

Contexts

—

Sometimes it is important to think 'out of the box' in relation to where work might be placed – or indeed, take place. Employment, postgraduate training and festivals are in many senses orthodox contexts where animation can be created and find a context for broadcast or exhibition, but there are further ways to think about using animation:

- Creating animation in a non-traditional context and relating to other disciplines or performance arenas.

- Using the materials created in the process of making animation, and images from the final film, as 'artworks' in their own right for display, dissemination (i.e., in educational contexts) and exhibition.

- Engaging with 'fan' cultures in the production, dissemination and appreciation of non-professional work, which gains its own 'artistic' or 'cultural' currency.

Art critic Jonathan Jones's claim that 'the most radical new idea has been of video and film installation as a genre in itself, independent of cinema, while seeming to fill the absence of an alternative culture of the moving image'[1] is especially extraordinary for two reasons. Animation has always provided an alternative culture of the moving image since its inception and it is strange to think that just because avant-garde 'film' projects have been placed in a gallery by named 'artists', this somehow invalidates all the experimental works played out in animation, which have not insisted upon their cross-disciplinary credentials and their status as 'art'.

An innovative animator, again reconciling traditional practice with new exhibition opportunities, Rachel Bevan Baker (see Chapter 13) has placed her work in a gallery space, but even this is not of a traditional order. Her project *Beaches* was already different in rejecting the often highly controlled studio-bound activity of much animation practice, by animating outdoors. This 'on-site' location work produced 11 short films, funded by a Creative Scotland Award from the Scottish Arts Council. Her work was presented in a travelling gallery that toured Scotland.

While Baker has exploited the Web to productive effect and the Web in general has become a comparatively new professional exhibition space (see earlier examples), another way it can be used for less aspiring, but nevertheless committed animators is in its 'fan' culture, and the activities emerging from 'amateur' or 'hobbyist' practices.

One of the most notable of these is the phenomenon of Legofilms. Karin Wehn, an academic at the University of Leipzig, Germany, has been engaged in research about this aspect of animation.

Wehn: 'This movement emerged independently in the mid-1980s and was not encouraged by Lego, but the company responded in 2000 by creating a Lego Steven Spielberg "Moviemaker" set, though it was not popular. It is a male-dominated community and it has embraced the easy principles of stop-motion to create work out of materials that are resilient, limited but accessible, and iconic. At a professional level, artists such as Michel Gondry have picked up on the phenomenon; he made a pixillated Lego pop promo for The White Stripes. There are now over 312 film-makers and 600+ films on the Lego website, and it is clear that from its small beginnings with film-makers like Dave Lennie and Andy Boyer, it is growing from an amateur practice into an art form in animation.'

NOTE

1. J. Jones, 'The Moving Image', Turner Prize Supplement, *The Guardian*, November 2003, p. 7.

22.4

Stills from a Lego walk cycle – Legofilms

Legofilms successfully illustrates how a fan culture can create a work that is both simple and sophisticated, offering an opportunity for the beginner and the advanced practitioner to make an accessible stop-motion animation. Every technique, however, has its walk cycle!

EXPERT ADVICE

Rachel Bevan Baker's advice for getting a film made:

- To keep things simple, don't try to squeeze a feature into a short film. It just gets messy. An apparently simple, short film can be full of ideas and meaning.
- Be honest and unpretentious.
- Think of the audience! Show your project to lots of people for feedback, right from the early stages of the idea.
- Don't give up on applying to film schemes/funders for money – the old saying of 'if at first you don't succeed, try, try again' is so relevant to getting funding or commissions these days! If your idea is good and you believe in it, you'll get it made. Every application and knock-back is useful in learning more about how to present your idea: maybe there are changes you could make to the way you present it; maybe you need to rethink audience/length/style. Listen to what people have to say. Be flexible.

Final Thought

—

All progress in any art form starts with someone saying 'What if?', and then seeking to play out an idea in the most practical and efficient way possible. Experience brings growth, and investment in research more understanding and improvement. It is hoped that this book has helped encourage and support animation practice in a number of ways and that students of all ages will benefit from it and progress the art further still.

Bibliography and Webography

Animation History

—

Adams, T. R. *Tom and Jerry: 50 Years of Cat and Mouse.* New York: Crescent Books, 1991.

Adamson, J. *Tex Avery: King of Cartoons.* New York: Da Capo, 1974.

Barrier, M. *Hollywood Cartoons: American Animation in the Golden Age.* New York and Oxford: Oxford University Press, 1999.

Beck, J. *The 50 Greatest Cartoons.* Atlanta: Turner Publishing Co., 1994.

Beck, J. *Animation Art.* London: Flame Tree Publishing, 2004.

Bendazzi, G. *Cartoons: 100 Years of Cartoon Animation.* London: John Libbey, 1994.

Brion, P. *Tom and Jerry: The Definitive Guide to Their Animated Adventures.* New York: Crown, 1990.

Bruce Holman, L. *Puppet Animation in the Cinema: History and Technique.* New Jersey: Cranberry, 1975.

Cabarga, L. *The Fleischer Story.* New York: Da Capo, 1988.

Crafton, D. *Before Mickey: The Animated Film 1898–1928.* Chicago: University of Chicago Press, 1993.

Eliot, M. *Walt Disney: Hollywood's Dark Prince.* London: André Deutsch, 1994.

Frierson, M. *Clay Animation: American Highlights 1908–Present.* New York: Twayne, 1993.

Holliss, R. and Sibley, B. *The Disney Studio Story.* New York: Crown, 1988.

Kenner, H. *Chuck Jones: A Flurry of Drawings.* Berkeley, CA: University of California Press, 1994.

Maltin, L. *Of Mice and Magic: A History of American Animated Cartoons.* New York: New American Library, 1987.

Manvell, R. *Art and Animation: The Story of Halas and Batchelor Animation Studio 1940–1980.* Keynsham: Clive Farrow, 1980.

Merritt, R. and Kaufman, J. B. *Walt in Wonderland: The Silent Films of Walt Disney.* Baltimore, MD: Johns Hopkins University Press, 1993.

Sandler, K., ed. *Reading the Rabbit: Explorations in Warner Bros. Animation.* New Brunswick, NJ: Rutgers University Press, 1998.

Art and Animation

—

Allan, R. *Walt Disney and Europe.* London: John Libbey, 1999.

Faber, L. and Walters, H. *Animation Unlimited; Innovative Short Films Since 1940.* London: Laurence King Publishing, 2004.

Finch, C. *The Art of Walt Disney: From Mickey Mouse to Magic Kingdoms.* New York: Portland House, 1988.

Gravett, P. *Manga: Sixty Years of Japanese Comics.* London: Laurence King Publishing, 2004.

Jones, C. *Chuck Amuck.* London: Simon & Schuster, 1990.

Jones, C. *Chuck Reducks.* New York: Time Warner, 1996.

McCarthy, H. *Hayao Miyazaki: Master of Japanese Animation.* Berkeley, CA: Stone Bridge Press, 2002.

Pointon, M., ed. *Art History* [Cartoon: Caricature: Animation], Vol. 18 No. 1, March 1995.

Russett, R. and Starr, C. *Experimental Animation: Origins of a New Art.* New York: Da Capo, 1988.

Wells, P., ed. *Art and Animation.* London: Academy Group/John Wiley, 1997.

Wiedemann, J., ed. *Animation Now!* London and Los Angeles: Taschen, 2005.

Withrow, S. *Toon Art.* Lewes, UK: Ilex, 2003.

Animation Studies

Bell, E. et al., eds. *From Mouse to Mermaid: The Politics of Film, Gender and Culture*. Bloomington and Indianapolis: Indiana University Press, 1995.

Brophy, P., ed. *Kaboom!: Explosive Animation from Japan and America*. Sydney: Museum of Contemporary Art, 1994.

Bryman, A. *Disney and His Worlds*. London and New York: Routledge, 1995.

Byrne, E. and McQuillan, M. *Deconstructing Disney*. London and Sterling: Pluto Press, 1999.

Canemaker, J., ed. *Storytelling in Animation*. Los Angeles: AFI, 1988.

Cholodenko, A., ed. *The Illusion of Life*. Sydney: Power/AFC, 1991.

Cohen, K. *Forbidden Animation*. Jefferson, NC and London: McFarland & Co., 1997.

Furniss, M. *Art in Motion: Animation Aesthetics*. London: John Libbey, 1998.

Hames, P., ed. *Dark Alchemy: The Films of Jan Svankmajer*. Trowbridge, UK: Flicks Books, 1995.

Kanfer, S. *Serious Business: The Art and Commerce of Animation in America from Betty Boop to Toy Story*. New York: Scribner, 1997.

Klein, N. *Seven Minutes: The Life and Death of the American Cartoon*. New York: Verso, 1993.

Lent, J., ed. *Animation in Asia and the Pacific*. London and Paris: John Libbey, 2001.

Leslie, E. *Hollywood Flatlands: Animation, Critical Theory and the Avant Garde*. London and New York: Verso, 2002.

Levi, A. *Samurai from Outer Space: Understanding Japanese Animation*. Chicago and La Salle: Open Court/Carus, 1996.

Leyda, J., ed. *Eisenstein on Disney*. London: Methuen, 1988.

Midhat, A. *Animation and Realism*. Zagreb: Croatian Film Club Association, 2004.

Napier, S. *Animé: From Akira to Princess Mononoke*. New York: Palgrave, 2001.

Peary, G. and Peary, D., eds. *The American Animated Cartoon*. New York: Dutton, 1980.

Pilling, J., ed. *That's Not All Folks: A Primer in Cartoonal Knowledge*. London: BFI, 1984.

Pilling, J., ed. *A Reader In Animation Studies*. London: John Libbey, 1997.

Pilling, J., ed. *Women and Animation: A Compendium*. London: BFI, 1992.

Sandler, K., ed. *Reading the Rabbit: Explorations in Warner Bros. Animation*. New Brunswick, NJ: Rutgers University Press, 1998.

Smoodin, E. *Animating Culture: Hollywood Cartoons from the Sound Era*. Oxford: Roundhouse Publishing, 1993.

Smoodin, E., ed. *Disney Discourse: Producing the Magic Kingdom*. London and New York: Routledge/AFI, 1994.

Stabile, C. and Harrison, M., eds. *Prime Time Animation*. London and New York: Routledge, 2003.

Wasko, J. *Understanding Disney*. Cambridge: Polity Press, 2001.

Watts, S. *The Magic Kingdom: Walt Disney and the American Way of Life*. New York: Houghton Mifflin, 1997.

Wells, P. *Around the World in Animation*. London: BFI/MOMI Education, 1996.

Wells, P. *Understanding Animation*. London and New York: Routledge, 1998.

Wells, P. 'Art of the Impossible', in G. Andrew, *Film: The Critics' Choice*. London: Aurum Books, 2001.

Wells, P. *Animation and America*. Edinburgh: Edinburgh University Press, 2002.

Wells, P. *Animation: Genre and Authorship*. London: Wallflower Press, 2002.

Animation Practice

Beckerman, H. *Animation; The Whole Story*. New York: Allworth Press, 2004.

Birn, J. *Digital Lighting and Rendering*. Berkeley, CA: New Riders Press, 2000.

Blair, P. *Cartoon Animation*. Laguna Hills, CA: Walter Foster Publishing, 1995.

Corsaro, S. and Parrott, C. J. *Hollywood 2D Digital Animation*. New York: Thompson Delmar Learning, 2004.

Culhane, S. *Animation: From Script to Screen*. London: Columbus Books, 1988.

Demers, O. *Digital Texturing and Painting*. Berkeley, CA: New Riders Press, 2001.

Gardner G. *Gardner's Storyboard Sketchbook*. Washington, New York and London: GGC Publishing, 2001.

Gardner, G. *Computer Graphics and Animation: History, Careers, Expert Advice*. Washington, New York and London: GGC Publishing, 2002.

Hart, C. *How to Draw Animation*. New York: Watson-Guptill Publications, 1997.

Hooks, E. *Acting for Animators*. Portsmouth, NH: Heinemann, 2000.

Horton, A. *Laughing Out Loud: Writing the Comedy Centred Screenplay*. Berkeley, CA: University of California Press, 1998.

Johnson, O. and Thomas, F. *The Illusion of Life*. New York: Abbeville Press, 1981.

Kerlow, I. V. *The Art of 3D Computer Animation and Effects*. New York: John Wiley & Sons, 2003.

Kuperberg, M. *Guide to Computer Animation*. Boston and Oxford: Focal Press, 2001.

Laybourne, K. *The Animation Book*. Three Rivers, MI: Three Rivers Press, 1998.

Lord, P. and Sibley, B. *Cracking Animation: The Aardman Book of 3D Animation*. London: Thames & Hudson, 1999.

McKee, R. *Story: Substance, Structure, Style and the Principles of Screenwriting*. London: Methuen, 1999.

Meglin, N. *Humorous Illustration*. New York: Watson-Guptill Publications, 2001.

Missal, S. *Exploring Drawing For Animation*. New York: Thomson Delmar Learning, 2004.

Neuwirth, A. *Makin' Toons: Inside the Most Popular Animated TV Shows & Movies*. New York: Allworth Press, 2003.

Patmore, C. *The Complete Animation Course*. London: Thames & Hudson, 2003.

Pilling, J. *2D and Beyond*. Hove, UK and Crans Pes-Celigny: RotoVision, 2001.

Ratner, P. *3D Human Modeling and Animation*. New York: John Wiley & Sons, 2003.

Ratner, P. *Mastering 3D Animation*. New York: Allworth Press, 2004.

Roberts, S. *Character Animation in 3D*. Boston and Oxford: Focal Press, 2004.

Scott, J. *How to Write for Animation*. Woodstock and New York: Overlook Press, 2003.

Segar, L. *Creating Unforgettable Characters*. New York: Henry Holt & Co., 1990.

Shaw, S. *Stop Motion: Crafts for Model Animation*. Boston and Oxford: Focal Press, 2003.

Simon, M. *Storyboards*. Boston and Oxford: Focal Press, 2000.

Simon, M. *Producing Independent 2D Character Animation*. Boston and Oxford: Focal Press, 2003.

Subotnick, S. *Animation in the Home Digital Studio*. Boston and Oxford: Focal Press, 2003.

Taylor, R. *The Encyclopaedia of Animation Techniques*. Boston and Oxford: Focal Press, 1996.

Tumminello, W. *Exploring Storyboarding*. Boston and Oxford: Focal Press, 2003.

Webber, M. *Gardner's Guide to Animation Scriptwriting*. Washington, New York and London: GGC Publishing, 2000.

Webber, M. *Gardner's Guide to Feature Animation Writing*. Washington, New York and London: GGC Publishing, 2002.

Whitaker, H. and Halas, J. *Timing for Animatio*. Boston and Oxford: Focal Press, 2002.

White, T. *The Animator's Workbook*. New York: Watson-Guptill Publications, 1999.

Williams, R. *The Animator's Survival Kit*. London and Boston: Faber & Faber, 2001.

Winder, C. and Dowlatabadi, Z. *Producing Animation*. Boston and Oxford: Focal Press, 2001.

Animation Reference

—

Clements, J. and McCarthy, H. *The Animé Encyclopaedia* . Berkeley, CA: Stone Bridge Press, 2001.

Edera, B. *Full Length Animated Feature Films*. London and New York: Focal Press, 1977.

Grant, J. *Masters of Animation*. London: Batsford, 2001.

Halas, J. *Masters of Animation*. London: BBC Books, 1987.

Hoffer, T. *Animation: A Reference Guide*. Westport, CT: Greenwood, 1981.

McCarthy, H. *Animé!: A Beginner's Guide to Japanese Animation*. London: Titan, 1993.

McCarthy, H. *The Animé Movie Guide*. London: Titan, 1996.

McCarthy, H. and Clements, J. *The Erotic Animé Movie Guide*. London: Titan, 1998.

Students can also consult the *Animation Journal, Animator, Animation, American Cinematographer, Sight and Sound, Screen* and *Film History* for relevant articles. There are also other titles purely dedicated to feature films, studio output and so on, which may also prove useful. Don't forget that books on comedy often have some information on cartoons etc. Similarly, 'readers' of essays about television etc. often have animation-related discussions.

Recommended Websites

—

Animation World Network: www.awn.com

Cartoon News and Discussion: http://forums.bcdb.com/

National Film Board of Canada: www.nfb.ca

Origins of American Animation: http://memory.loc.gov/ammem/ oahtml/oahome.html

UK Animated Cartoons Reference: www.toonhound.com

US Animated Cartoons Reference: www.toonarific.com

Many of the suggested texts also have lists of links for all aspects of animation from practice tutorials to festivals to archives to research and study.

Index

Acknowledgements and Credits

Acknowledgements

—

Paul Wells

I would like to thank the following people for their help in the creation of this book:

Brian Morris, Natalia Price-Cabrera and Renee Last at AVA Publishing SA, without whom the first edition of this book would never have existed. Suzie Hanna, for work over and beyond the call of duty – many thanks! Andy 'Harry Tuttle' Chong and Ben Dolman, for unfailing technical and moral support – always appreciated. All my colleagues at Loughborough University School of Art and Design, Kerry Drumm, for helping out quickly at the start, Simone Potter (BFI), Jackie Leonard (Brownbag Films), AJ Read (Cosgrove Hall), Richard Barnett (Slinky Pictures), Tina Ohnmacht (FilmAkademie), Avrim Katzman (Sheridan College), Chris Williams (University of Teesside), Mark Walsh (PIXAR), Helen Cohen (SilverFox), Graham Ralph (SilverFox), Sarah Woolway (BBC), Andy McNamara (BBC), Siddiqa Juma (Aladdin Media), Dick Arnall (Animate!), Hélène Tanguay (NFBC), Shelley Page (DreamworksSKG), Louise Fletcher (Blue Sky Resumes), Mette Peters (Netherlands Institute of Animated Film), and, of course, all the talented named contributors within the text.

Samantha Moore

I would like to thank the following people:

Georgia and James at Bloomsbury for their patience, help and support. Paul Wells for asking me to be part of this book. Everyone who agreed to have their beautiful images included, and was kind enough to grant interviews. Joanna Quinn, consistently generous and unfailingly kind, for providing the amazing cover images. The staff and students at Wolverhampton University, School of Media, particularly Emily Mantell and Ross Winning, for their support and encouragement. The staff and students at Loughborough University Animation Academy. Jonathan, Stan and Archie Bates for being wonderful, and providing chocolate. Finally, my mother, Jennifer Moore, for everything.

Credits

—

Front Cover: Beryl and letters courtesy Joanna Quinn / BAF / National Media Museum

1.1–1.3: Images courtesy of Paul Driessen

2.1: Image courtesy of Amblin / Universal / The Kobal Collection
2.2: © Joanna Quinn
2.3–2.4: © Iain Gardner
2.5–2.7: © Richard Phelan
2.8–2.11: © Second Home Studios 2011
2.12: Images courtesy of Silver Fox Animation LLP and Dreamworks Animation
2.13: © Aardman Animations 1989
2.14: Images courtesy of Silver Fox Animation LLP and Dreamworks Animation
2.15: Studio Kresceneho / A Loutkoveho Filmu / The Kobal Collection
2.16: © Bill Plympton
2.17–2.18: The Brothers McLeod Ltd
2.19: © Richard Phelan
2.20–2.21: The Brothers McLeod Ltd
2.22: © Brown Bag Films
2.23: © Goddard / Brown Inc.

3.1: Star Film / The Kobal Collection
3.2: Images courtesy of Chris Shepherd and Maria Manton
3.3: DFGW / COI / Maria Manton / Chris Shepherd
3.4: Images courtesy of Chris Shepherd and Maria Manton
3.5: Images courtesy of Aaron Bradbury and Chris Gooch

4.1–4.2: Millimages S.A. / Zoo Lane Productions Ltd / La Cinquième
4.3: © Christa Moesker
4.4: Steve May / TalkBack Productions
4.5: Millimages S.A. / Zoo Lane Productions Ltd / La Cinquième
4.6: © Aardman Animations 1989

5.1: New Line Cinema / The Kobal Collection
5.2: Warner Bros / The Kobal Collection

6.1: The Animation Academy

8.1: Vitagraph / The Kobal Collection
8.2: Winsor McCay / The Kobal Collection
8.3: Aurica Finance Company / Black Ink / Fritz Productions / Steve Krantz Productions / The Kobal Collection
8.4: Akira Committee / Pioneer Entertainment (USA) Inc. / The Kobal Collection
Walk Cycle Tutorial (pp.111–14): Arril Johnson
8.5: The Animation Academy
8.6: Courtesy of Kingston Museum
8.7: Image courtesy of the Department of Transport / COI / Darcy / Maria Manton / Chris Shepherd
8.8–8.9: Yamamura Animation

9.1: RKO / The Kobal Collection
9.2: Image courtesy of Wladyslaw Starewicz Productions / The Kobal Collection
9.3: Columbia / The Kobal Collection
9.4: Dreamworks / Pathé / Aardman Animations / The Kobal Collection
9.5–9.6: Images courtesy of Barry Purves
9.7: Images courtesy of Timon Dowdeswell
9.8: Philips Broadcast / Philips Company Archives
9.9–9.14: Photo by Katarzyna Sejud

10.1: Images courtesy of Dave Johnson

11.1–11.2: Images courtesy of Michael Frierson

12.1: Walt Disney Pictures / The Kobal Collection
12.2: © 1991 STUDIOCANAL FILMS LTD. All Rights Reserved / The Kobal Collection
12.3: Lorimar / Universal / The Kobal Collection
12.4: © Media Molecule
12.5: © Seed Animation Ltd
12.6: Images courtesy of Studio AKA / eOne 2008
12.7: Images courtesy of Chris Landreth
12.8–12.9: © BBC Scotland / Designer: Paul Kavanagh Studio
12.10–12.14: Images courtesy of Anja Perl and Max Stolzenberg
12.15: © 2009–2015 Rovio Entertainment Ltd. Rovio, Angry Birds, Bad Piggies, Mighty Eagle and all related titles, logos and characters are trademarks of Rovio Entertainment Ltd. All Rights Reserved.

13.1: Courtesy of the British Film Institute
13.2–13.3: © Elizabeth Hobbs
13.4–13.7: Images courtesy of Maureen Selwood

14.1: Jewel Productions / The Kobal Collection
14.2: © Samantha Moore

15.1: Images courtesy of Studio AKA / Woolley Pau
15.2: Images courtesy of Studio AKA / Orange Telecommunications / WCRS
15.3: Images courtesy of Studio AKA / Marc Craste

16.1 Images courtesy of Michal Pfeffer and Uri Kranot

17.1: Image courtesy of Aardman Animation
17.2: Images courtesy of Blue Sky Resumes

18.1: Images courtesy of Ugly Studios Ltd / Imprint Studios
18.2–18.3: © Brown Bag Films

19.1: © Second Home Studios 2012
19.2: © Second Home Studios 2011

20.1: © Bill Plympton
20.2: Images courtesy of Michal Pfeffer and Uri Kranot

21.1: Images courtesy of Michal Pfeffer and Uri Kranot
21.2: © Holly Rumble

22.1: © Gwénola Carrère
22.2: © Anima Mundi
22.3: Image courtesy of Peter Parr
22.4: Nick Maniatis – Brick-Tastic! Films